MUCH SILENCE

Meher Baba: his life and work

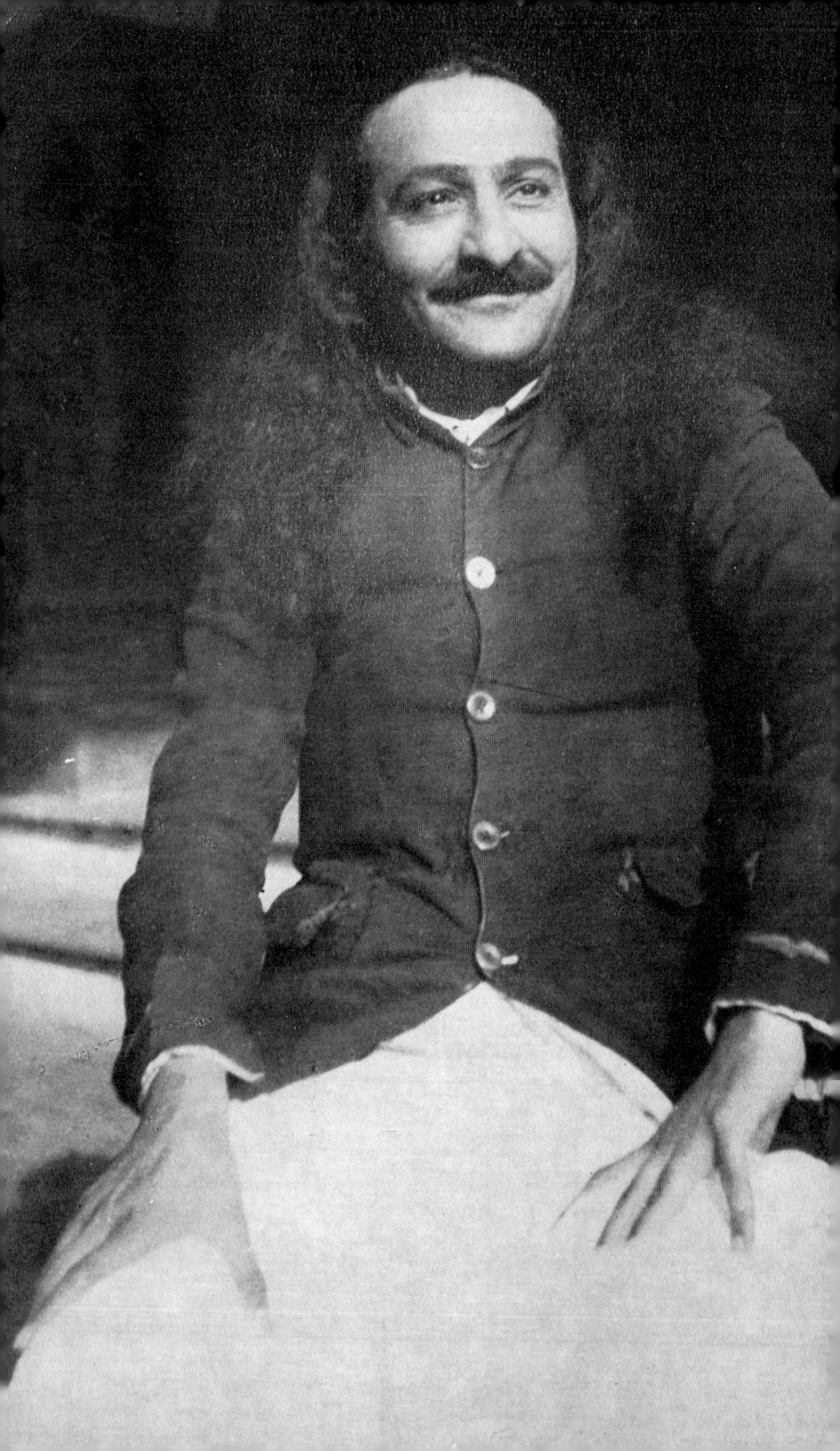

MUCH SILENCE

MEHER BABA: HIS LIFE AND WORK

by

Tom and Dorothy Hopkinson

LONDON
VICTOR GOLLANCZ LTD
1974

© Meher Baba Spiritual League Ltd 1974
© Copyright in the Talks and Discourses of Meher Baba belongs to Adi K. Irani

ISBN 0 575 01410 5

MADE AND PRINTED IN GREAT BRITAIN BY
THE GARDEN CITY PRESS LIMITED
LETCHWORTH, HERTFORDSHIRE
SG6 1JS

"Much silence makes a mighty noise."
AFRICAN PROVERB

"When mankind becomes completely deaf to the thunder of his silence, God incarnates as man."
MEHER BABA

ACKNOWLEDGEMENT

A NUMBER OF books have been written about Meher Baba, apart from those dictated by himself or consisting of extracts from these dictations. Many are listed at the back of this book, and anyone wishing to know more about Baba's life and work can learn from them as we have done. But hitherto there has been no short record, covering the whole period of Baba's earthly life, written in language the man in the Western street can readily understand and without assuming knowledge he is not likely to possess. That is what this book is intended to provide.

To do this we have depended heavily on what has already been written, and though we have drawn a great deal from many sources, we must stress our special obligations to the following works, and our thanks to the copyright holders for permission to make quotations. *The Perfect Master* by C. B. Purdom (Williams & Norgate Ltd, 1937); *The God-Man* by C. B. Purdom (George Allen & Unwin Ltd., 1964); *Avatar* by Jean Adriel (J. F. Rowny Press, Calif., 1947); *Meher Baba, Family Letters, 1956–1969*, by Manija Sheriar Irani (Soc. for Avatar Meher Baba, New York, 1969); *Listen, Humanity* by Meher Baba, narrated and edited by D. E. Stevens (Dodd, Mead & Co., New York, 1957); *God Speaks: the Theme of Creation and Its Purpose* by Meher Baba (Dodd, Mead & Co., New York, 1955); *Discourses* by Meher Baba, published in India, 1939, and now out of print; also in London, as *God to Man and Man to God* (Victor Gollancz Ltd, 1955); and in the U.S.A. *Discourses by Meher Baba*, edited by Ivy Oneita Duce and Don E. Stevens (Sufism Reoriented, 1967); *The Wayfarers* by William Donkin, with a foreword by Meher Baba (Adi K. Irani for Meher Publications, India, 1948); *Meher Baba's Last Sahavas* by Dr H. P. Bharycha (published by himself from Navsari, India, 1969).

We are also grateful for permission to quote from MSS notes "I Remember . . ." by Delia de Leon, and must acknowledge our debt to the three magazines currently devoted to Meher Baba, *The Glow, The Awakener* and *Divya Vani*, which have been invaluable for checking and amplifying the record of the books. Details of these magazines are included in the bibliography.

T. and D. H.

CONTENTS

Part One: His Life

Chapter		page
1	Meeting Meher Baba	13
2	Early Life	21
3	Intense Activity	30
4	The 'Thunderous Silence'	40
5	Travel in the East	47
6	Travel in the West	54
7	Bringing East and West Together	62
8	The 'God-Intoxicated' (1)	68
9	The 'God-Intoxicated' (2)	76
10	'Helpless and Hopeless'	85
11	The 'Great Personal Disaster'	96
12	The Avatar	105
13	A 'So-Called Tragedy'	112
14	The Long Seclusion	123
15	The Last Sahavas	133

Part Two: His Teaching

	Introduction	145
16	The Drama of the Ego	147
17	Sex, Marriage and Love	154
18	The Soul's Journey Through Creation (1)	165
19	The Soul's Journey Through Creation (2)	172
20	The Journey Home	184

Part One:
His Life

Chapter 1

MEETING MEHER BABA

WHAT IS THE purpose of man's life on earth? How does he come to be here? What happens to him when he dies?

Are his ideas of right and wrong rooted in reality? Or are all morality and ethics merely part of social custom, varying with place and time? And if so, how is man to guide his life by anything more lasting than convention and self-interest?

Does human nature progress in any real sense? Are human beings today 'better' than human beings of a thousand or ten thousand years ago? Are we any more able than they were to live in peace, developing our natures and talents to the full? Or have we, instead of becoming wiser and more understanding, merely become more complex and more knowing?

Is man intended to be happy—and if so, why is he everywhere so miserable and so mean? We all assume happiness to be the end of life, we are all, in our own ways, pursuing happiness throughout our lives—then why do we never overtake it? Which one of us all in his secret heart considers himself happy? Which one of us believes those about him—his wife and children—to be happy? How many of us, looking honestly around, can say that we know one truly happy man, or—rarer still—a happy woman?

In every age man is haunted by these questions. No access of power or accumulation of possessions, no degree of absorption in his occupations, no abandonment to pleasure ever entirely drives them from his mind. And when we are old, or sick, or poor, or impotent, or deserted—the unanswered questions force themselves upon our notice, and we realise, when it seems too late to do anything about them, that they were of more concern to us than all the activities on which we are spending or have spent our lives.

There are moments in most lifetimes when we ask ourselves if we have been travelling in the wrong direction, and whether the ideas about life which we took over from those about us were as foolish and misdirected as their own lives are seen to be. At such moments, for an instant, we may even be ready to make changes in ourselves and in our way of life, if we could believe such changes would give us the happiness we seek.

But who can give us such a guarantee?

Being creatures of our age we perhaps look first to politics and science. But while politics can make the external conditions of life fractionally more just and less oppressive, it can do nothing to relieve our inner state. Changes in the political system may ensure that men have enough to eat, are decently housed and their children educated, that they do not suffer avoidable ill-health or die sooner than they need—but we know that, when all such necessary changes have been brought about, man will only have acquired better surroundings in which the same anxieties, frustrations, agonies must still be faced.

Has science anything to offer to the purpose?

Most Westerners have a split attitude to science. On one level we regard science as 'God' and count on it to solve all problems. Science should be able, we believe, to control the dangerous elements in our environment, preventing floods and famines, forestalling earthquakes, eliminating accidents and modifying the harshness of the climate. It should multiply crops, develop new sources of food and energy, invent machines to do arduous and dirty work, and so abolish poverty and toil. Through drugs or techniques, already available or still to be discovered, it should free us from infirmity and disease, alleviate anxiety and mental stress, and greatly extend the span of human life. Science should —surely indeed before long it will—enable every one of us to live a hundred and fifty or two hundred years, free from pain or distress of any kind.

However, science also offers us another face, so that while we look trustingly to it as our all-providing father, we also fear and distrust it as the Great Destroyer. Not only has science, and its pillion-rider technology, put into our hands the means to destroy our planet with devices such as bombs and gases which we all recognise as deadly, but in a strange way the good and evil faces of this deity keep interchanging. Pesticides to improve our crops, detergents that help wash our clothes and dishes, plastic containers that keep food clean and fresh—all useful, seemingly benevolent inventions—produce together a problem of pollution by which our world is overwhelmed. And those 'conquests' over disease, those rising living standards, that lengthening of the span of life, have together landed us into the nightmare of overpopulation. If we call in science to deliver us, which face is it going to show? And if it takes away certain of our problems, what fearful new anxieties will it hand us in return?

So then we come, however reluctant, to religion and religion is ready with answers to all our questions. That is, after all, its business—to know the future, and to interpret the past and present. Religion will never say that it 'doesn't really know', 'can't understand', or that it hopes to have the answer in a century or two. Religion will tell us how we can be happy, and happy under all conditions. It tells us why we came here, how to live while we are here, what happens to us when we die. Nor is it the case, as men often claim—being eager to find reasons for not following difficult advice—that religions speak with conflicting voices and recommend opposite courses of action to us. Far from it. In their essential message all great religions speak as one; they tell us that the aim of life is to know and love God, and that the way to do this is to love and serve our fellowmen, putting their happiness and wellbeing before our own.

But just as science has a double face, so has religion. Preaching on one side, practice on the other, and man judges religions not by what they say but by what they do, their actions rather than their claims. And we see that religious bodies which preach poverty have amassed enormous wealth, and while preaching humility exercise worldly power. The greater part of mankind professes one great religion or another, yet, while all insist on the brotherhood of man, their followers wage wars and kill each other—counting up the dead with satisfaction—for material and political advantage, or for belonging to a different creed. Sometimes indeed for belonging to another branch of the same creed, so justifying Jonathan Swift's bitter words that "we have just enough religion to make us hate, but not enough to make us love one another." And this is done not by primitive, underdeveloped peoples but by those who consider themselves the leaders of civilised mankind—and we are all involved in the killing and the hypocrisy, or have been at one time or another.

Whether a man were born a Buddhist, a Jew, a Moslem, a Christian or a Zoroastrian would not matter at all, if he *lived* his religion he would find it impossible to kill his fellowmen, or to enrich himself through other men's ignorance or weakness. Holding fast to the same truths, in whatever words they might be expressed, he would pass his life without surrendering to worldly values, but equally without withdrawing into monasteries or caves. He would not escape suffering but would understand it, and would learn from what he suffered. Through understanding, and through serving his fellowmen—without expecting gratitude for doing so—he would find, first, tranquillity of heart and mind, and, later, the glow of inner happiness. And he would find this not in a distant heaven but here on earth.

However, we live in a different world from that of the first Christians, facing problems they never envisaged and could not comprehend. Just as they too lived in a different world from India in the time of Buddha, or Persia in the days of Zoroaster. Lasting truths, if we are to recognise and accept them, have to appear in contemporary dress, restated afresh for every age in terms of man's current knowledge and the problems of his situation and environment.

The writers of this book believe that such a restatement of lasting truth in reference to the contemporary world has been made in our own day by Meher Baba, who was born in 1894 and whose earthly life ended in 1969. This belief is the result, first, of having met Baba and the lasting effect of that experience; second, of the study of his life and writings. Baba refused to found any religion, saying that we have been given all the religions we require, and for the last forty-four years of his life he never spoke, since what man needs, he pointed out, is not more words but to pay attention to those which have already been spoken. He came, he said, not to teach but to awaken.

But today the words which Baba did not speak, and the Discourses which were not uttered but dictated by means of an alphabet board or with signs and gestures, are finding their way into men's hearts and minds. Not only into the hearts and minds of those who, having once met him, can never forget that experience, but even more into the hearts of those who never saw him, particularly of the young. And Baba's appearance, unknown to newspaper readers or television viewers, is familiar to them from the sleeves of records or the pages of the underground press.

Meher Baba was of medium height, about five feet six. As a young man his build was slender, and films show him moving with a graceful, floating walk—with which he many times covered thirty miles a day, for days on end, so that his most vigorous companions could scarcely keep pace with him. Later, after his two severe car accidents, his body became thick, since almost any form of movement gave him pain; but when you put your arms round him—for he would often embrace his followers or allow them to embrace him—his body seemed simultaneously firm and insubstantial, as though having solidity but little weight. As a rule he wore Indian dress with sandals or else with his feet bare, and since they were almost never confined in shoes, his toes stood out separate and strong. His hands looked powerful enough to crack stones, but he moved his fingers with astonishing delicacy, as though playing an invisible musical instrument, to convey his silent meaning; while doing so he would often look up at his interpreter with a humorous, trustful gaze. His expression changed continually, but it was particularly through his eyes that the pattern of thought and feeling was conveyed. Intensely black, they would in a few seconds lovingly greet his audience, sparkle with laughter, or contemplate some situation with a sternness there was no resisting or escaping. When you yourself became the object of a particularly penetrating gaze, it became impossible to return the stare, so that one turned one's head aside like a cat or dog looked directly in the eyes by a human being.

At different periods Baba wore his black hair at varying lengths, down to his shoulders and below in early life; later short and brushed back from his high square forehead; braided at times into a pigtail. He had a powerful hooked nose, giving him in one or two photographs the look of a Kurdish brigand, and his skin—which was neither dark nor fair but something in between, as might be expected from his Persian origins—was unusually sensitive. This sensitivity compelled him when in the West to be careful about cold or draughts; while in India he took care, at least in later life, to protect head and face with an umbrella or shady hat.

Simply to come into Baba's presence was for most people a profound experience. Some, on first seeing him, burst into tears. Some flung, or tried to fling themselves at his feet, an attempt which those about him were ready to forestall. One or two laughed hysterically. Many found themselves smiling with a happiness they could not explain, but which to their own astonishment they did not try to hide. Almost all, whatever the anticipations with which they had approached him, found it difficult, even painful, to leave his presence.

What made the experience memorable and any description of it difficult, is that Baba had not—like royalty, or most political and religious leaders—a set reaction, even a gracious and dignified reaction. He responded to every individual afresh, giving himself in contact. So it was as if to each man or woman who approached him, he embodied something that person had been waiting for throughout his or her life. What is it we have all, each one of us, been waiting for throughout our lives? An intense experience of love. Meher Baba radiated love so that it appeared to even a casual visitor as though Baba loved him or her in some quite special way.

Once over the first reaction to his presence, it was noticeable that Baba seemed far more alive than anybody else. In any crowd, however large, he was invariably the centre, and everyone in it was governed by the same impulse, to get near enough to see and make contact with him. A film, made in the 1950s in the U.S.A., shows Baba in a crowded dining-room of men and women seated at small tables. Roving from group to group, he has the effect of a lamp carried round a darkened room. As he approaches a table, the sitters raise their heads, gaze up, animate, smile—and then, as Baba moves on, they dwindle down, relapsing into the zombie-like condition normal to us human beings after he has passed.

Baba was never frivolous or flippant, but he disliked needless solemnity; he loved jokes and entertaining anecdotes, which those about him would save up for his enjoyment. At the 1958 gathering of his followers at Myrtle Beach in the U.S., following some profound discourses, Baba asked: "*Now*, what do you want? One more discourse, or music and jokes? Personally, I want jokes, but let's keep your wish. I want you all to be happy. . . ." Among those close to him Baba kept a special place for one Kaka whose flow of inconsequential chatter, expressed in a confusion of languages invented by himself, provided a daily entertainment and distraction.

An aspect many found surprising was Baba's utter absence of self-importance, and refusal of special treatment. He lived austerely, took only the plainest food, invariably travelled by the cheapest class. Except on the rarest occasions he would never allow outward signs of reverence such as bowing or kissing his feet. In November 1962 when the whole *mandali*,* or group of close companions, bowed solemnly before him, they recalled with astonishment that this was the first time for twenty-two

---

* A Sanskrit word meaning a group or company. As with other words which he took over, Baba gave this one a special significance.

years they had been permitted to do this. Baba himself, however, frequently bowed down, and those to whom he bowed were the poor, the afflicted, such as lepers, and the unappreciated. During a visit to the United States in 1952, it was noticed that Baba remained seated as he always did when people were brought to meet him. But each time a black family or person entered, he stood up.*

An immense dignity surrounded Baba, and an authority which could in a moment overawe aggression or hostility, but in general his manner was disarming. Even while remaining seated, he came out to welcome you. Unlike those spiritual leaders who cultivate aloofness and permit faint contact to be effected through a haze of condescension, Baba would often express a childlike candour and simplicity, against which the armour of the sophisticated offered no protection.

"And what have *you* come here for?" he enquired, turning towards a journalist who had been watching his interviews with others.

"I only wanted to see you," the journalist replied, caught off his guard and using the first words that came into his head.

Baba flung up his arms with a delighted smile, as though no reason could be more acceptable, and asked: "And do you *like* me?"

To his surprise the journalist—who knew little about Baba and nothing about his teaching—found himself struggling to bring out the words: "I love you". Failing to conquer his English inhibition, he managed at last to bring out... "Yes... I like you."

"And I like you", Baba smilingly replied, and touched his visitor's forehead.

In this brief contact, as in thousands of others, Baba showed his power to cut directly through the artificial personality we all construct for self-protection in our daily lives, and reach that inner self which lives on somewhere in us all. "When I am with Sadhus" (holy men) he said once, "no one is more serious than I. When I am with children I play marbles with them. I am in all, and one with all. That is why I can adapt myself to all kinds of people, and meet them where they are."

Baba's sister, Mani, in her delightful 'Family Letters',† tells

---

* 'Memories of '52' by Filis Frederick. *The Awakener*: vol. XIV, No. 2.
† *Eighty-Two Family Letters*, written by Mani (Manija Sheriar Irani). Society for Avatar Meher Baba, New York, 1969.

of a man who came to see Baba with a long list of questions he was determined to have answered. Baba motioned the visitor to sit beside him, and he sat there quietly taking in Baba's presence —and only on leaving did he confess the intention with which he came, and which till now he had forgotten.

Quentin Tod, an actor who was one of the first Westerners to become attached to Baba, described his meeting with him in London in 1931. "What impressed one most was his rather wild quality, as of something untamed, and his truly remarkable eyes. He smiled and motioned me to sit beside him. He took my hand and from time to time patted my shoulder. We sat for several minutes in silence and I was aware of a great feeling of love and peace emanating from him; also a curious feeling of recognition came to me, as if I had found a long-lost friend."

Before going to meet Baba, Tod said, he felt unprepared and shaken "as though about to undergo a major operation." But what impressed him and many others, once they came into Baba's presence, was just the opposite of fear, the sense of being accepted as one is and for what one is, this acceptance being conveyed by an embrace, a touch on the face, a taking of the hand on arm. Soothed by this acceptance, the timid cease to feel exposed; the desperate sense a trickle of new hope; the worldly, the resentful, the self-occupied, instead of feeling guilty, experience intense relief, because for the first time someone is seeing us as we are, and has understood at a glance how we have come to be like that.

Chapter 2

EARLY LIFE

MEHER BABA MEANS 'compassionate father', Meher being an adaptation of the name Merwan which formed a part of Baba's full name—Merwan Sheriarji Irani. He was born at Poona in India of a Persian family on the 25th February, 1894, at 5.15 a.m.

At that time Baba's father, Sheriarji, was already in his middle fifties. From the age of thirteen Sheriarji had been a seeker after spiritual truth, roaming the country as a monk or dervish, first in Persia and then in India. Failing to achieve the enlightenment he sought, he visited the home of his sister in Bombay, who urged him to marry and bring up a family. It is said that a dream or inner voice assured him that one of his children would achieve what he had not, by becoming a great spiritual leader. "There was none like him," Baba said. "It was because of him that I was born as his child." Sheriarji followed his sister's advice and took a wife, a girl in her teens known as Shirinbanoo or Shirinmai, settled down and set himself to earn a living. As a child he had received no education, but he now started to educate himself. Even while working as a gardener, later as an estate manager and teashop owner, he learned to read and write four languages and gained a reputation as a poet and singer.

Shirinbanoo, unlike her husband, was an educated woman, "as intelligent as she is fair," said one of her friends. Merwan was her second son, born when she was only sixteen years old, and the home to which she brought him from the Poona hospital was a small house of two rooms, plus kitchen, bathroom and garret, which her husband had bought and repaired. Here Baba grew up with an older brother and three younger ones and his sister Mani, another sister having died at the age of six. The family moved for a couple of years into a flat, but then came back to a larger house in the same street as their first home.

Shirinbanoo later told of her many worries over her precocious son. "Merwan has been my problem even as a child... he was very active and mischievous from the time he was able to toddle, and would walk out of the house when my attention was distracted. This often compelled me, when I was especially busy with housework, or had to go for my bath and there was no one in the house to look after him, to tie one end of my sari to the waist and the other to the bedstead. Even then I could not always keep him out of mischief. Once (this was about January 1895, when Baba was not yet one year old), I had left him playing on the floor. Returning to the room some minutes later I was horrified to see him playing merrily with a big black snake (a cobra). I rushed forward, but the snake slipped quickly out of the house and was never seen again."

To most English people the name 'Poona' suggests an India of garden parties and polo-playing subalterns, but in fact Poona, which stands on the junction of two rivers, is an important cultural and educational centre. It had been chosen as the seat of the Bombay government because, though no more than 120 miles away, it offers a far pleasanter climate during the hot seasons, being 2,000 feet above sea level. From the point of view of schooling, the family was extremely well placed; Merwan began attending school at the age of five and at fourteen entered what was considered to be the best in Poona, St Vincent's High School (Roman Catholic) from which he matriculated three years later.

His childhood was a happy one. Untroubled as yet by a sense of his own destiny, he was lively and mischievous, though naturally gentle and unselfish. He took great pleasure in games, particularly hockey and cricket (he was a batsman and wicket-keeper) and long after he ceased to play would enjoy watching cricket matches. His sister Mani recalls him saying on busy days that there was this and that to be done when he "would much rather be watching a game of good cricket." The boy was also a good runner and strong walker—as his companions learned later in life during their immense journeys over the Indian countryside.

In his studies he is said to have been quick to learn, methodical and punctual. This is easy to believe since later in life he was punctual to the minute and insisted that every task had to be tackled in the most practical, economical way. His special interest was in poetry. Besides reading widely he wrote poems in English, and also in Gujerati, Urdu, Persian and Hindustani. Some were printed in a Bombay newspaper, and at the age of fifteen he had a story published by his favourite boys' adventure magazine—the *Union Jack* of London. But just as avidly as poetry he read detective magazines and Edgar Wallace stories, and one of his earliest followers, Ramju Abdullah, recalled many years later that what had first drawn him to Baba was a common enthusiasm for Sexton Blake. Merwan was also intensely fond of music, loved singing and had an exceptionally sweet voice. "He had a rich juicy voice" was how one of his mandali, Adi K. Irani, long afterwards described this.

Once school was over Merwan's enjoyments were like those of other boys. A couple of elderly Parsis kept a small shop near St Vincent's and the old lady often gave cold drinks or handfuls of sweets to Merwan and his friends. The old man, with his eye on the profits, would chase them away from the front of the shop, and the kindly old lady would beckon them round to the back. A photograph of this time (1907) shows a boy with brooding eyes and a full-lipped humorous mouth; he wears a trim dark jacket, with tucks in the sleeves to be let out as he grows taller, and what seems to be a school badge is pinned to the pocket. His hair, which would later become black, was at this time reddish-gold.

Merwan had one habit, however, not usual among boys of twelve or thirteen, he was fond of solitude and would slip away by himself to sit for hours at the 'Tower of Silence'. Both his father and grandfather had been keepers of the Zoroastrian 'Tower of Silence' in the Persian village where they lived, and now young Merwan found the tower near Poona his natural retreat for silent contemplation. These towers, on which the Zoroastrians expose their dead in gratings to be devoured by vultures, caused horror among early Western travellers brought up to regard burial in the earth as the only proper way to dispose of bodies, even though it meant setting aside large tracts of useful land in which the dead, after a more or less expensive funeral, can decay slowly over the years in the dampness of the soil. Moreover to Christians, believing in only a single life on earth, there was comfort in the thought of their bodies staying on in the village or town where they had spent their lives. But the Zoroastrians consider exposure of the dead as the method best suited to their arid climate, in which vultures are the natural scavengers. It is also the one least costly or harmful to the interests of the living; and, as believers in reincarnation, they regard the body as little more than a coat which the individual has made use of, as it were, in passing. Towers of Silence are built away, but at no great distance, from towns and villages, and often in situations whose wide outlook over the countryside, combined with the purpose for which they were built, might well induce profound reflections in a meditative mind.

At the age of seventeen, a new period opened in the boy's life. Not far from Poona was Deccan College, at which Sir Edwin Arnold* and other distinguished men had been professors. The finest educational institution in the province, it was one of the few which already, in the days before the First World War, allowed some liberty to its students.

Merwan entered Deccan College in 1911. Here, as at school, it was above all literature to which he was attracted. He read Shakespeare, Wordsworth, Shelley and many other poets, English, Indian and Persian; but the poet with whom he was enraptured and continued throughout his life to quote—for Baba possessed the faculty of recalling almost everything he ever read —was Hafiz, one of the greatest of Persian lyric poets, whose work expresses the most profound spiritual longing in the language of passionate love.

During his first year, Merwan passed his examinations with credit, and was active in social life. Here, as at school, he was accepted as a natural leader to whom others went for advice, or called in to arbitrate in their disputes. Outside College, he founded The Cosmopolitan Club. Its rules, which forbade quarrelling, gambling and bad language, might be thought naive. But there was nothing naive about the insistence in its constitution that anyone might belong regardless of community and caste—an attitude far in advance of the time.

In Merwan's education, therefore, East and West were blended, Western schooling against a background of the East, with studies and fluency in several languages, and this may have helped to evoke early in life the resolution to bring people together, without regard to race or creed or class or colour. During his second year at Deccan College, however, an event happened, outwardly of small significance, but which put an end to Merwan's studies, disrupted what had been hitherto a conventional and happy life, and set on foot the transformation of his whole nature through the intensest suffering. This was an encounter with an aged woman named Hazrat Babajan. At the time of the encounter she was said to have lived already for one

* Author of *The Light of Asia*.

hundred and twenty-two years, and in other ways also she was no ordinary old woman.

Hazrat Babajan had been born in about the year 1790 in the mountainous country of Baluchistan to the west of India, daughter of one of the chief ministers to the Amir of Afghanistan. Exceptionally beautiful, she was due to be married as a girl of fifteen, but was already overwhelmingly drawn to the spiritual life. Rather than marry, she disappeared from home and had already spent half a century of wandering before she found a Master, through whom at the age of sixty-five she achieved the complete spiritual enlightenment she had always sought—a state to which the term 'God-realised' is applied, meaning that she had realised to the full the divine aspects of her nature and now lived continually in the enjoyment of God's presence. A Moslem by religion, she went in 1903 on a pilgrimage to Mecca, appearing around 1907 in Poona, where she made her home under a neem (lime) tree in what was known as the Malcolm Tank Road. It is not uncommon in India to see holy men dwelling in the roots of trees which they have adapted to form shelters. Babajan, however, built no shelter for herself but simply perched, exposed even to the drenching storms of the monsoons, with merely some sacking as protection. Only ten years before her death in 1931, did her disciples with great difficulty obtain permission from the authorities to construct a small shelter for her, which, since Babajan refused to move, had to be built around the tree. Objection was based on the fact that her neem tree stood at a busy crossroads, so that the thousands of pilgrims who came to gaze at her, to kiss her hands, or to escort her on her daily walk to the garden in which she would sit for some hours looking out over the river, caused dislocation of the traffic.

At the time of the encounter with Merwan, however, there was no shelter, and Babajan was sitting in her tree on the morning in May 1913, when the boy came riding home from college on his bicycle. As he passed the tree he looked up and their eyes met. He knew quite well who she was, and when she beckoned to him he went over to her and she kissed him between the eyes. No word was spoken, and after sitting with her for a short time, Merwan remounted and road home. From that day he would go every evening to sit with Babajan, usually without a word exchanged. "I was drawn to her," he later said, "as steel to a magnet." And whenever he spoke of her he would use the words "matchless", "incomparable". He often also referred to her as

'Emperor', and it is noteworthy that she herself took the name Baba (father) Jan, and would flare up if anyone addressed her as Amma (mother) Jan, since women are held to be the weaker sex and God-realisation is not for weaklings.

So their silent meetings continued, and then one night in January 1914, Babajan was in more talkative mood. As Merwan, having kissed her hands, stood humbly before her, she pointed her little finger at him and uttered the words: "This child of mine will after some years create a great sensation in the world and do immense good to humanity." This powerful assertion, following the many hours of silent contact between them, had a shattering effect.

For some moments Baba remained standing before her, and then went home. It was late and he went straight to bed. Hardly had he lain down before he began to suffer alarmingly; through his body passed what seemed to be fierce electric shocks, causing him agony mixed with an intense joy. Before long he lapsed into unconsciousness, and when his mother found him on his bed next morning his eyes were vacant, he was unable to move or speak, and she supposed he had been taken seriously ill. Not until the fourth day did he show any recovery of consciousness and then remained for nine months in a state which amounted to continual trance, showing no interest in his surroundings and no inclination for food or drink. Whatever was put before him he gave away to beggars or dogs, or put it into some drawer where it went bad and stank. He appeared never to sleep, and if he embarked on any action would be liable to continue it for hours in complete unawareness of the outside world.

Once, leaving his home to go to the Bund Garden, he walked there and back three times without a pause, a distance of fifteen miles. He stayed for three days lying down near his old haunt, the Zoroastrian Tower of Silence. His parents became desperate. They supposed he had "gone out of his mind", and he was placed under medical treatment, but the sleeping draughts and morphia injections given to him had no effect. Many years later Baba spoke to some of his followers about his experiences at this time:

> When I was a boy I did not know anything. I had nothing to do with spirituality... I preferred games...
>
> One day, when a friend gave me a small booklet on the Buddha, I opened the book to the place that told of the second coming of the Buddha, as Maitreya, the Lord of

Mercy, and I realised all of a sudden, 'I am that, actually', and I felt it deep within me. Then I forgot about it, and years passed by. Babajan called me one day as I was cycling past her tree; she kissed me on the forehead, and for nine months, God knows, I was in that state to which very, very few go. I had no consciousness of my body, or of anything else. I roamed about taking no food. My mother thought I was mad, and called the doctor. My father understood, but said nothing. The doctors could not do anything.... I took no food but tea, which my elder brother Jamshed, who loved me very much, gave me. One day, all of a sudden, I felt nature's call. I wanted to move my bowels, but it was impossible because I had not had any food. I sat there and had no stool. Then I saw, with these gross* eyes of mine, circles and circles, whole universes. From that moment, instead of the Divine Bliss that I was in, for nine months I was in such tortures that none in the world can understand. I used to bang my head to relieve my pain. I scarred my head on floors and walls.† I could not contain myself. It was as if the whole universe was on my head. I used to break windows open with my forehead.... My sleepless, staring, vacant eyes worried my mother most... In her anguish she could not refrain from going once to Babajan and demanding to know what she had done to me... Babajan indicated to my mother that I was intended to shake the world into wakefulness, but that meant nothing to Shirinmai in her distress.

This condition of acute suffering persisted until November 1914, when some degree of normal consciousness began to return. Baba later explained that the kiss given him by Babajan had carried him into the bliss of God-realisation, and that the intensity of his sufferings was due to unwillingness to come down into normal consciousness, which was essential for the work he had to do. Babajan herself used to quote to Merwan certain Persian lines which mean: "Having gained freedom, you have come back as prisoner (to free others)." Merwan's eyes now gradually ceased to be vacant and he started to take small quantities of food; he had become, he said, "like an automaton possessing

* 'gross' i.e. physical, as distinct from inner perceptions.
† The house and the room, known as 'Baba's Room' in which he used to hammer his head on a stone in the floor, can still be seen. It is the second, larger house, number 765, in the section Butler Moholla, where Baba grew up, and which has now been renamed Meher Moholla.

intuition." At this moment a friend brought along a poor young man, Behramji Irani, later to become one of Baba's most devoted followers, to whom he offered to teach Persian. Behramji made rapid progress, and Merwan's parents, delighted, tried to get him to accept other pupils, which he refused though continuing to instruct Behramji.

As Merwan's hold on life strengthened, he felt an impulse to travel, and particularly to visit the homes of great saints or sadgurus. It was in this way that he came, in December 1915, to visit the temple of Khandoba where a renowned saint and master, Upasni Maharaj, had been living for three years on water, having been reduced by his fasting almost to a skeleton. Upasni Maharaj was no less remarkable a being than Hazrat Babajan. By religion he was a Hindu, a tall heavy man, usually naked except for a gunny cloth and sandals when he went out. He had a lowering look and piercing eyes. His behaviour was often strange and sometimes appeared to be mad. He once lived for over fourteen months in a bamboo cage, only three by three and a half feet, taking nothing but coffee once a day. Two years after Merwan's first visit to him he became a Perfect Master, the highest of spiritual states, and on his death in December 1941, the village where he lived became a place of pilgrimage. The part Upasni Maharaj played in Baba's life was a decisive one, and Baba has left his own account of their first meeting.

> When I came near enough to him, Maharaj greeted me, so to speak, with a stone which he threw at me with great force. It struck me on my forehead exactly where Babajan had kissed me, hitting with such force that it drew blood. The mark of that injury is still on my forehead.... With that stroke Maharaj had begun to help me return to ordinary consciousness.

As Merwan's mind began to focus more directly upon everyday life, his mother insisted that he should take up some employment, and in 1916 he joined a theatrical company as manager. But when before long the owner died he was glad to come back to Poona. Here he was put in charge of his father's teashop, and later of a toddy or palm-wine shop. In neither capacity was Merwan a success, being always more concerned with meeting people's needs than with taking payment for what they had received. And in the toddy bar he would often urge the drinkers, usually among the city's poorest people, to drink only moderately or give it up altogether. However he applied himself wholeheartedly to all menial labour, washing up bottles, cups and dishes, sweeping the floor, washing over the tables and benches.

From the day when he had been struck with the stone by Upasni Maharaj, Baba started to revisit Babajan with whom he would sit for about an hour each evening. He went almost daily also to the Parsi Tower of Silence or wandered on into the jungle beyond, where he would repeatedly knock his head against stones, wrapping his brow with a handkerchief to conceal the bruises from his family. Twice a month he visited Upasni Maharaj with whom he also exchanged letters, none of which unhappily have been preserved. Finally in July 1921, Merwan, now three-fourths normal in behaviour, went to live for six months with Upasni Maharaj at Sakori. They would spend a number of hours each day together, and sometimes whole nights behind closed doors which no one was permitted to approach. As a rule they sat in silence, but sometimes Merwan would sing. By the end of that year Merwan had recovered full consciousness and Upasni Maharaj solemnly handed over authority to him. He instructed his own disciples, much as John the Baptist did with Jesus, to leave him and stay with Merwan for the future: "I have given my charge to Merwan. He is the holder of my key." Later he stated publicly: "This boy will move the world. Humanity at large will be benefited at his hands." He referred to Merwan as 'the Sadguru* of this Age', and told Behramji: "Your friend is God-realised. Carry out every command and every desire of his." Finally he himself addressed Merwan by the title 'Avatar'.†

So now, at the age of twenty-seven, Merwan Irani had become Meher Baba and was ready to begin his life's work for mankind.

* A Sadguru is a man who has become one with God, but remains on earth for the help and guidance of others. He is also known as a 'Perfect Master' of whom there are said to be five on earth at any one time.

† The Avatar is not man become God, but God become man. The best-known and most accepted manifestations have been as Zoroaster, Rama, Krishna, Buddha, Jesus and Mohammed.

Chapter 3

INTENSE ACTIVITY

HAVING RECEIVED RECOGNITION as Perfect Master from the hands of other Perfect Masters,* Baba withdrew for a period of concentration before launching out on a life of intense activity. For this purpose he left his parents' home and went to live in a hut only six feet by ten, inadequate even for a monastic or prison cell, which he asked a friend to build for him. He has described this period of his life himself:

> For about four months [January–May 1922] I stayed in a small *jhopdi* [thatched hut]. It was built for me temporarily on the edge of some fields in what is now the Shivajinagar area of Poona. In this manner I began to live independently surrounded by men who formed the nucleus of the mandali. One of these was the first to start addressing me as 'Baba'. Some of the men were drawn intuitively to me before they had any clear idea of my inner state. Others were attracted to me by hints from Babajan and Maharaj. And still others I drew directly to me.

Asked why he chose to confine himself to such cramped quarters, Baba replied: "It does not inconvenience me, for walls do not bind me. For certain kinds of work which I have to do in non-physical realms, I prefer to shut myself up in a small place." And throughout life, when the nature of such work demanded it, he would instruct his followers to construct a small hut, or sometimes to find and prepare a cave, in which he remained closeted for a period ranging from hours to weeks. Often

---

* There were five concerned in the 'appointment'. Besides Hazrat Babajan and Upasni Maharaj, these were: Tajuddin Baba, once a soldier in the service of the British. On attaining God-realisation, he gave up his military calling: 30,000 were said to have been present at his funeral. Sai Baba was the master of Upasni Maharaj, to whom he directed Meher Baba. The fifth, Narayan Maharaj, lived as a rich man in a large well-furnished bungalow. They were thus three Moslems and two Hindus, one woman and four men.

the site chosen would have special associations with a Master or holy person from the past, and once in Italy he spent a night and a day fasting in a cave near Assisi which was associated with St Francis.

Meantime Baba was making contacts among young men in the neighbourhood who, beginning as friends, transformed themselves before long into disciples, and it was with a group of forty-five of these that in May 1922 he set off on foot from Poona to Bombay. Twelve of them were Moslems, eleven Zoroastrians like Baba's own family, and the rest Hindus. On reaching Bombay Baba rented a large bungalow which he named Manzil-e-Meem (The Master's House), where he established his first *ashram*. There were fifteen rooms, but there was to be no furniture; only blankets were allowed for bedding, without bedsteads, mattresses or quilts. Each morning the men went out to work at various employments, but in the evening they had to come straight home, and their life was governed by strict rules to which—as to any instruction from the Master—absolute obedience was required.

All must retire to bed by 8.0 p.m. and be up each morning at 4.0 a.m., since the early hours are best for prayer and meditation. Before this they had all to take cold baths, including even a sufferer from asthma, who found to his surprise that after a while he had lost his asthma. Meals were vegetarian, but all were obliged to eat heartily of the simple food except during periods of fast. Drink and sexual intercourse were forbidden. Anyone going out off duty must leave purse and money behind, and while on duty not more than two annas (twopence) might be spent on refreshment, a sum which at that time would have paid for tea or a cold drink. All earnings went into a common fund for the benefit of all, and no one was allowed to own any personal possessions. Each man was instructed to keep the holy days and religious observances required by his own religion.

But though the regime was strict, life in the ashram was far from gloomy. Baba was fond of all kinds of games, for which regular times were allotted, and of music and singing. He often took his followers to the theatre and cinema. Free speech was encouraged and the group had its own governing body at which the members were expected to speak out freely. The same practice was encouraged by Baba's habit of suddenly asking a follower to say exactly what was in his mind—a technique familiar in the West to students of psychology—and at breakfast he would often ask one or another to recount his dreams.

It was understood among Baba's followers that he never allowed life to settle into a fixed pattern; the unexpected was always just around the corner. On one occasion Baba ordered followers who were then fasting to collect two hundred beggars at the ashram. There is never any shortage of beggars in Bombay, but Baba did not want sturdy able-bodied rogues, only the truly suffering or disabled. When gathered together, bathed and clothed, Baba himself took part in serving them and even, to their astonishment, garlanded them before they left. Another time, when the whole party was subsisting on nothing but water, Baba ordered no fewer than eight hundred beggars to be assembled, fed and clothed, but this time the able-bodied might also be included. Once, possibly because of some murmuring over the simple fare, Baba chose half-a-dozen of the mandali for whom he ordered a feast to be served. The half-dozen were delighted to be given fresh and dried fruits, bowls of chocolates and the rich sweetmeats so much loved in India. But when they had already eaten heartily, cooked dishes appeared and the Master heaped their plates, and when these dishes were followed by still others, the disciples begged for mercy.

Often Baba's demand for strict obedience led one or other of the men into an awkward situation. Those who went to work each day could speak to their colleagues in factory and office or to their fellow-disciples, but were forbidden to speak to anyone else. One worker travelling home by train in the evening found himself face-to-face with an old schoolfriend, to whose warm enquiries he offered no answer but an embarrassed stare, which he maintained until he reached his station and could thankfully escape. Painful as such incidents were at the time, the mandali came to understand that every demand or instruction had a purpose. Unlike those who spend their lives in monasteries or convents, Baba's followers were being trained to live in the world but maintain detachment from it. The breaking of social ties might be a necessity for one pledged to live by different values. The ability to fast and go short of sleep, the capacity to travel around—and perhaps even assemble a group of strangers—without money for fares or transport, would prove invaluable to them later on, developing qualities of determination and initiative without which they could never have faced their arduous life as Baba's close companions. From the physical point of view

* *

they underwent the equivalent of a rigorous military discipline and training. At times they came in for some rough handling as well.

"My body," Baba explained,

> was then very lean, but also supple, as I was constantly and energetically active. From four in the morning even in the severest cold I would move about in my thin mull *sadra* [robe]. Those who did not know me well at that time might have considered me very quick-tempered, for suddenly, with or without provocation, I would beat anyone at hand.
>
> In those days most of the mandali were hefty, robust young men. Several of them were good wrestlers and some were seasoned athletes. But when I would start for a brisk walk, the majority would have to run to keep up with me...
>
> One of the group had the physique of a giant, but once in a certain mood I knocked him down with a single slap. Another had to have a doctor treat his ear because of a blow I gave him. One of the mandali used to go into hiding on such occasions and would not emerge again without asking others if my mood had changed.

Strange as such actions seem to us, a similar fiery phase of activity is commonly understood and accepted by the followers of Eastern masters. Like the abuse they sometimes shower on their disciples or on one another, it is the outward manifestation of an inner purpose which is always beneficial, and a sharp blow from a Perfect Master—like the blow from a stone which Baba himself received from Upasni Maharaj—is often the means of conferring spiritual enlightenment. So, too, a rebuke from a Master is a favour. Appreciation of this was shown by a Sanskrit research scholar whom Baba rebuked at one of the *sahavas*, or public gatherings. Afterwards he said gratefully: "Ah, Baba must really love me, otherwise he would not have taken the trouble to correct me."

Two members of the mandali who continued with Baba throughout his life left memories of these early days. One, Sarosh,* was asked by Baba to join his ashram. With some hesitation he agreed to try it for a year and 'see how I get on.' However he was continually finding himself in situations in which he had somehow disobeyed the Master, and when he got back

---
* His full name was Sarosh K. Irani. He died in 1973.

would find his bedroll thrown out of the house. Distressed, he would then plead with Baba to be allowed to bring the bedroll in and resume his place among the group. Eventually Baba would agree, embrace Sarosh, and all would go on as before—until again he found his bedroll outside the door.

Sarosh was a lively, good-looking youth with social interests, so this may have been Baba's way of forestalling any idea on his part of leaving the ashram. If so, it was well calculated, for Sarosh, who had signed on reluctantly for twelve months, remained for life. With Baba's approval he later married, founded a successful motor-car business and became Mayor of Ahmednagar. With his wife, Villoo, he several times served as Baba's ambassador on official occasions, and their home has given a welcome to scores of Baba's followers from all over the world.

Another early member was Meherjee (Meherjee A. Karkaria) who joined Baba as a boy of eighteen. He remembered Baba, who occasionally used to smoke at this time, giving him a single puff of a cigarette. When he had taken it, Baba told him to take another puff. He then ordered: "You are never to smoke again. But this," indicating a drink by a gesture of his arm, "is all right for you." Meherjee, who is sometimes troubled with his throat, considers this was a practical warning for the good of his health. He too married with Baba's approval, and later it became important for him to establish some kind of business. Baba told him to go into the making of filter papers for use in industry. Meherjee hardly knew what filter papers were, and had no idea how they were made. His factory now employs two hundred workers, is the only factory of its kind in India, and saves the country large sums in foreign exchange.

The house Manzil-e-Meem had been rented for a year. However on the last day of March 1923, when there were still two months left to run, Baba called the mandali together. He told them the ashram was to be wound up. He would be leaving for Ahmednagar shortly, taking only a few of them with him. The rest should go to their homes, from which those who wished could join him later. But he warned them to think well before doing so since "discipline will be more strict and the mode of living more simple ... you may have to do the work of masons, of coolies; in short, any kind of manual work."

Meanwhile, for Baba and the few remaining with him, there ensued a period of continual travel. The little band was always on the move, ranging the country and travelling once as far as Persia. Often they went on foot, if by boat or train it was always in the lowest class, which Baba insisted on throughout his life. Apart from unavoidable privations of living on the march in a country of desert, mountain and forest with extremes of temperature, they were frequently under orders to fast; Baba himself fasted often, and once took nothing but liquids for two months on end—and this while walking across the continent with each man carrying his own bedding roll and equipment. The places where they put up were always the poorest and cheapest, and the men's tempers were constantly being tried by abrupt changes of plan. Hardly had they settled into some shelter, hoping to stay here for a while and recuperate, than they were ordered to pack everything together and be ready to move off next morning, or possibly in the middle of the night. They existed like soldiers on campaign, but without a soldier's usual reliefs of grumbling and getting drunk.

In the course of their travels, Baba led his band to a little walled town called Arangaon, not far from Ahmednagar. This was an ancient settlement, now decayed into ruins, among which a number of peasants, mainly so-called 'untouchables', were living in poverty and degradation. 'Degradation' is no fanciful description since the filth of their clothes and persons was extreme, and their way of life almost brutish. They were accustomed, for example, to eating the bodies of any dead animals they found. Close by the old town was a dilapidated military camp, a hang-over from the First World War. Yet this was the spot chosen by Baba to bear his name and become permanently associated with his life and work as 'Meherabad' ('abad' means flourishing). Like other places chosen by Baba, it had spiritual associations from the past. Here was the tomb of Buaji Bua, a Hindu saint who was said to have entered his grave while still alive. It had also been chosen for burial place by a Moslem saint, Hazrat Shah; when the saint's followers remonstrated with him for choosing a spot so desolate and barren, he replied: "You are wrong; this will blossom into a place of unique importance and thousands will visit it.... So it is ordained, and so it shall be." It was here then that in March 1924, twelve months after leaving Manzil-e-Meem, Baba founded his second ashram.

Life at Meherabad was just as strictly disciplined as in Bombay and the diet equally sparse, but now in addition there

was the heavy manual work he had warned them of a year ago
The men had to clear the ground, put into order whatever buildings could be made serviceable, and start constructing new ones. The first to be built resembled the hut in which Baba had lived at Poona, being a small, square room—solidly built of stone and mortar and rendered insect-proof with screens—to which Baba could retire for periods of solitude. Apart from one paid mason, everything was done by the mandali, whose numbers had risen again to about forty, and who toiled away as labourers for six hours each day. After some months, under Baba's direction, they had covered the abandoned camp with a whole range of buildings. Looking back years later on the scene, Baba recalled:

... it was like a small model town. In it lived about 500 souls, working in the hospitals, the dispensary and the schools. There were also ashrams for boys, men and women, and shelter for the poor and for lepers.... At that time nearly a thousand rupees a day used to be spent for the maintenance of the various services, while the mandali often lived on plain dal [curried vegetables] and rice for lunch, and milkless tea or a thin soup of methi [bitter spinach] leaves and coarse bread for dinner.... I remained generally on liquids or on limited meals taken once in a week or a fortnight.

Weekly rations were issued to the most helpless of the Arangaon villagers. They were so needy that later, when the ashrams were shifted some scores of miles away to Toka, they used to travel on foot or by bullock-cart the whole distance rather than miss the weekly quota of coarse grain.

Hundreds of people from the villages near Meherabad benefited from the free hospitals, and thousands utilised the dispensary provided for outpatients. Boys of all castes and creeds including untouchables soon began to live, eat and intermingle freely....

From dawn to dusk I would move about the place and take an active part in every phase including the cleaning of latrines.* Each day I spent three to four hours bathing the school children. When the number boarding became considerable, I allowed the mandali to share this service with me. All the mandali also had to grind grain for one to three hours

---

* In this way Baba was doing for 'untouchable' children the very work of latrine-cleaning and refuse clearing which caused these children, and the class from which they came, to be classed as 'untouchable'.

each day, depending upon their assigned duties. I also shared in the daily grinding for an hour or more.

The school children to whom Baba refers were attending a free primary school which was among the other new institutions. Starting with 20 boys, it had soon grown to take in 150 boys and girls, among whom were about 30 untouchable boys from poor and squalid homes, and it was these whom Baba spent so much of his time washing and bathing. At first they had been segregated, but it was not long before all differences of caste and creed were broken down and the children accepted one another freely.

Once when Baba was engaged in the bath-house, some high-caste Brahmins called to receive his blessing. As they stood before him, Baba told them: "I am bathing untouchable boys. It is no use having my blessing unless you are prepared to do the work I do." The Brahmins set aside their code, according to which it is defilement even to be crossed by an untouchable's shadow, and joined Baba in his task.

If the Bombay ashram resembled a monastery whose inmates were seeking enlightenment by living under discipline while working in the world, the ashram at Arangaon wore rather the aspect of a social centre whose efforts are directed towards serving the community. And if the motivation of the first was Eastern and spiritual, that of the second seemed practical and Western. Life in Bombay had been a form of seclusion with outside contacts strictly limited, but to Meherabad vast crowds were now starting to flock in. Sometimes the stream flowed on all day, and on Baba's thirty-second birthday, 25th February, 1926, some 20,000 people gathered to receive his *darshan* (blessing). Some were indeed seekers after truth, but most—as Baba observed to the mandali—were really intent, despite their protestations, on getting some material advantage. Baba spoke of these with humorous tolerance:

> Once an old man offered to dedicate everything he had to me, and then he would begin, he said, to lead a life of service and renunciation. However, on investigation it was found that what would be dedicated to me was a wife and seven children to be taken care of....

Another who came asking for divine guidance was advised to remain with Baba and lead the life of an ascetic. He did so for ten days, but then said he must be off. Enquiry showed that what he did not care for was the food. Baba let him go, with only a comment to the mandali: "Came for God, and gone for bread!"

A third who approached in tears declared: "For forty years I am in search of God. I do meditations; now I come to you!" Baba answered, "If you obey me, I will give you God-realisation. What about obeying?"

"I will cut off my head," the man declared, "and lay it at your feet!"

"You need not cut off your head, but be stark naked and walk about Ahmednagar."

The man, who was well-dressed, objected: "Baba, that is very difficult, for I was brought up here. I know many people. What will they say?"

"If you cannot do this," Baba replied, "why talk of cutting off your head?"

Despite the almost ceaseless activity of his daily life, it was at this period that Baba wrote a book, which has never been published and which no one, so far as is known, has ever read. He wrote it in various places, partly in his hut, partly at a seat under a neem (lime) tree by the roadside, and partly in a hut up on the hill in another part of the Meherabad settlement. To this book—which is said to contain Baba's message to the world, including spiritual secrets which have never been revealed—Baba devoted some hours of each day for about a year, usually sitting down to write at six in the morning behind closed doors, and sometimes continuing far into the night. At times he became so exhausted that he had to be massaged with oil before he could continue, and once he had a severe attack of fever lasting nearly a week, but he always went back to his task.

One of the mandali, Meherjee Karkaria, remembers that the book was written in English in Baba's own longhand. In early days he took it with him everywhere. Housed in a steel box with chain and padlock, it travelled all over the sub-continent and possibly overseas as well. Meherjee recalls it many times being pushed under Baba's seat in crowded railway carriages. Later it was kept in a bank vault, from which it is known to have been collected in 1956 by a devotee now dead. "No one," it is said, "knows where the book is now." But somebody in fact must know, or be going to know, for when Baba was asked, in the month before he laid down his body, where the book might be found, he replied: "It is all right, and you are not to worry. It is being looked after."

One day in October 1926, when the centre's activity was at its height, Baba called a special meeting of the mandali and put to them his proposal. All the work which had been built up with so much effort over the past two and a half years, should now be wound up, and the buildings, with only two or three exceptions, levelled to the ground. The mandali naturally expressed concern at the prospect of up to four hundred people being left helpless and homeless, but it was soon clear that Baba had thought out all arrangements, and no person who needed relief was left without it. However, a work seemingly of great value to the community, work on which much effort and money had been spent, was brought to an abrupt stop.

Few aspects of their work with Baba were more puzzling to the mandali than the rapidity—it sometimes seemed to them the capriciousness—with which Baba put a stop to one kind of activity and directed all their energies and his own into something different. Baba's own comment was: "Usually a temporary scaffolding is set up around a big building which is under construction, and when the building is completed, the scaffolding is removed. Often my external activities and commitments are only the outward expression of the internal work I am doing. The school, hospital, etc., were but scaffolding for my real work.... Hence, when my work is finished, I have no need of scaffoldings."

Another time he declared: "I have not come to establish retreats or ashrams. I create them for the purpose of my universal work, only to repeatedly dissolve them once that purpose has been served.

"The universe is my ashram, and every heart is my house...."

This is an attitude hard for most Westerners to accept. We are accustomed to think of hospitals and schools as 'absolute goods', which should continue indefinitely and if possible expand. But for Baba his model town, like other activities he would start and then wind up, was only the shell for work of universal application. Its main importance was invisible and symbolic—for the mandali it also provided a lesson to be learned. But there were other lessons, and only so much time could be given to each. No one around Baba would be allowed to settle into a routine, even a routine as beneficent as handing out grain and bandages and washing the untouchables.

Chapter 4

THE 'THUNDEROUS SILENCE'

WHEN BABA DREW to an apparent end the work at Arangaon—much of which would be resumed in one way or another before long—he inaugurated a new period, one of intense travel all over the sub-continent, leading up to a period of wider travel which would carry him and some of the mandali all over the world. But before considering that, there is another, and a particularly mysterious, aspect of Baba's life and work to take into account; from as far back as 10th July, 1925, Baba had spoken no single word.

Shortly before the end of June in that year, Baba informed the mandali that he would observe a long period of silence. This was to begin on the 1st July, but as the day neared, Baba postponed it till the 10th, telling them that the silence then begun would last for a whole year. At the end of this time he would "come out into the open", an expression which some took to mean a final manifestation, after which there would be no further use for worldly goods or possessions. One went so far as to give away all his belongings and urge his family to do the same. The women disciples simply could not believe that Baba actually intended to keep silence for a whole year, and comforted one another: "At the most, he will keep silence for one month." And when, on the evening of the 9th July, Baba said, "Hear well my voice: you will not hear it for a long time," no one about him, man or woman, dreamed that the Master's silence would last, not for one year or five or ten, but for more than forty-three years, and be still unbroken when his earthly life came to an end.

Why did Baba undertake his silence? Speech is the precious means of communication which above all distinguishes man from animals. On speech and writing the whole of man's intellectual development is based. To become dumb or deaf, and so cut off from easy communication with others, is thought of as one of

THE 'THUNDEROUS SILENCE'

the greatest disasters that can happen to a man. Why did Baba bring this seeming disaster on himself?

It is true that after some years several of the mandali, in particular Eruch,* became so adept at interpreting Baba's meaning, that a few rapid gestures, illuminated by Baba's astonishing range of facial expression, enabled them to convey long explanations and instructions. Even a newcomer, watching Baba's face and hearing the quiet voice of Eruch close beside him, came away with the sense of having carried on a full conversation—and only later would recall that Baba himself had uttered no word. But during those first years when his voice would be most missed by his companions, Baba had to resort, first to a slate or writing pads, and then from January 1927, when he gave up writing as well as speech, to the laborious use of an alphabet board. This too, many years later in October 1954, would be discarded, after which only hand signs would be used. Surely, it might be argued, Baba was placing a needless burden on himself and a handicap on his work, by the avoidance of speech. Certainly among Western intellectuals the idea of a Master who did not speak seems to arouse particularly angry disbelief, as though Baba were in some way criticising all talkers by his silence.

Of the silence Baba himself said:

I have come not to teach, but to awaken. Understand therefore that I lay down no precepts.

Through eternity I have laid down principles and precepts, but mankind has ignored them. Man's inability to live God's words makes the Avatar's teaching a mockery. Instead of practising the compassion He taught, man has waged crusades in His name. Instead of living the humanity, purity and truth of His words, man has given way to hatred, greed and violence.

Because man has been deaf to the principles and precepts laid down by God in the past, in this present Avataric form I observe silence. You have asked for and been given enough words—it is now time to live them.

Baba's silence therefore served to impress upon the world that he had not come to add one more to the list of the great religions which man persistently misunderstands and distorts, using them

* Eruch Jessawala, whom Baba called "My right hand".

to sanctify the self-interest, greed and hatred they were intended to help him overcome. Baba realised very well that if he put forward any 'new religion', it would inevitably go the way of all the rest. The very people who accepted the new teaching would take it over and 'interpret' it, so that inevitably it would be brought down by degrees to the level of the interpreters, and forced to conform to the attitudes and interests of mankind in general. With the 'teachers' would come 'organisers' who would codify and structure the new religion, place it on a sound financial footing and equip it with churches, temples and a hierarchy of priests. It would then compete for converts with other religions, measuring success by the hundreds of thousands who showed up at its services, the extent of references to it in newspapers or television programmes and the number of noughts in its bank balance.

With none of this would Baba have anything to do. He was as scathing about church organisations as Jesus was about the scribes and Pharisees, or as he himself was later on about the "hypocritical saints and masters that now flourish everywhere like poisonous mushrooms", masters who travel in their own Rolls-Royces and own vast tracts of real estate. Instead of putting forward a competing religion, Baba called attention through his silence to the underlying truth which is the same in all religions, and by means of which, he said, he would one day draw all religions and creeds together "like beads on a string."

We spoke above of speech and writing as factors on which "the whole of man's intellectual development is based." And this may itself have been a powerful reason for Baba's keeping silent, since his message was not to man's mind but to his heart, and the heart can only be reached when the mind is by-passed or induced to abdicate its dictatorial role. To a great gathering of his Eastern followers at Poona in May 1965, Baba gave this message:

> This time of your being with me, I do not intend giving you a lot of words to exercise your minds. I want your minds to sleep so that your hearts may awaken to my love.
>
> You have had enough of words, I have had enough of words. It is not through words that I give what I have to give. In the silence of your perfect surrender, my love which is always silent can flow to you—to be yours always to keep and to share with those who seek me.

When the Word of my Love breaks out of its silence and speaks in your hearts, telling you who I really am, you will know that this is the Real Word you have been always longing to hear.

At another time, on the same theme of the limitations of mind, he made the dry comment: "To ask for a purely intellectual proof of the existence of God is like asking for the privilege of being able to see with your ears."

At different times Baba gave other explanations for his silence, not different but related to those given above. He said that he undertook it partly to assist him in carrying out his spiritual work, and partly because of the wars, upheavals and catastrophes which he saw coming upon the world and particularly on India, the land where he had chosen to live.

Neither of these statements can be easily understood since we have no conception of what the spiritual work of a great master can be, even less than we can conceive—for example—what goes on in the mind of a great physicist or composer. But we can perhaps accept that Baba's silence, like the seclusion into which during the latter part of his life he withdrew for months on end, made possible a conservation of energy which he applied to far more potent effect than if he had dissipated it in words—of which already "you have asked for and been given enough." Energy retained he could make 100 per cent use of because he exercised 100 per cent control over it; energy discharged in speech must depend on the use the listeners made of it, we listeners who have already shown ourselves "deaf to the principles and precepts laid down" throughout eternity.

One consequence of Baba's silence, much feared by those about him at the outset, did not eventuate. A loss of contact and intimacy with the mandali and others close to him might have been expected when the Master no longer spoke directly to them. Yet surprisingly the opposite was true, for Baba did not adopt a reserve or maintain a stony speechlessness. On the contrary, he gave himself through his ever-changing facial expressions; through his eyes which saw without illusion and yet radiated love; and through the forceful gestures of his hands and fingers. Moreover the very fact that he did not speak compelled all who came into contact with him to concentrate their full attention in the effort to comprehend what he was seeking to convey. And the combination of silence with this dynamic visual expression produced on even casual visitors the awe-inspiring sense of a Being living simultaneously in the finite world and in the infinite.

Yet when all explanations have been sought, there remains a profound mystery about Baba's silence, and a further mystery attaches to the statements he made from time to time about the breaking of it. These were full of promise, repeated in varying words throughout his life, sometimes in general terms, at others with specific dates. "I am silent. My Silence is not merely an observing of silence. My Silence has a purpose behind it. When I break it, all will know. The breaking of my Silence will be as forceful as thousands of atom bombs exploding together."

And again: "This idea of the self as a limited, separate entity will vanish. Co-operation will replace competition; certainty will replace fear; generosity will replace greed; exploitation will be no more. When I speak, I will reveal the one supreme self which is in everyone."

In the same Universal Message we have already quoted, beginning with the words, "I have come not to teach, but to awaken", which was delivered on the 10th July, 1958, the twenty-third anniversary of his silence, Baba went on to say that the time for breaking his silence was near, and that he must complete everything within six months from the 14th July.

"When I break my Silence, the impact of my Love will be universal, and all life in creation will know, feel and receive of it. It will help every individual to break himself free from his bondage in his own way. I am the Divine Beloved who loves you more than you can ever love yourself. The breaking of my Silence will help you to help yourself in knowing your real Self..."

When he spoke so often of breaking his silence, and of the One Word which he would utter and of its universal impact, was Baba talking in the terms of normal human speech or of his own inner language? Following the sahavas which he held in September 1954, he made a statement on the distinction between the two. Baba had spoken of "the destruction of three-fourths of the world" and emphasised that this had been said "in my own 'language' alone".

"It is," he said, "really very difficult for anyone to believe and understand what I say, because none can grasp the meaning underlying my words.... Everyone is free to interpret my words in any way they think or feel. But one thing I tell you, that whenever I say a thing, I naturally use my own 'language' and whatsoever is said by me is truth. But my 'language' is such that none can understand or grasp the underlying meaning of what I say; therefore, when I want to say a thing I have simultaneously to make use of your language also, knowing well that you would understand nothing whatsoever if I were to make use of my 'language' alone." And he went on to clarify which of the statements in his 'Final Declaration' had been made in terms of normal speech, and which in his own 'language', or in both. The possibility therefore remains that Baba's words about the breaking of his silence were in his language not in ours.

Persons closest to him seem to have accepted this as explanation. In 1960 Baba had said that he would end his silence, but did not. Eruch then commented: "The delay that we feel to be made by Baba in carrying out His word is but the reflection of the delay within us in our preparedness to accept His Word of words."

And in June 1963 Baba's sister Mani wrote in her 'Family Letter': "We who are with Baba are understandably not excited when the Beloved pinpoints a time when He says He will break His silence. Those concerned most with Him, are somehow least concerned about when He will break it."

Finally there are many followers who believe that Baba did in his own way 'break his silence', either shortly before or at the moment when he laid down his earthly life. They believe this because they experience his presence even more closely today than they did while he was still on earth. In Eruch's words: "He seems to have come into their hearts more forcefully than ever before. They feel His presence without seeing Him, and I can quite believe that, because I too feel that way. Although I miss Him, I feel His presence without seeing Him—the same as when Baba used to send me away on some errand, He being where He was."

To sum up, there is an apparent contradiction in Baba's repeated statements that he would shortly break his silence. Those who were closest to Baba worry about this least. Those who are now his followers either feel that he has spoken to them, or that he postponed his speaking for good reason, or that he used the word 'speaking' in his own personal language.

Perhaps every Avatar leaves a mystery for man to think over. Buddha left a mystery in the manner of his death. Jesus left the mystery of his Second Coming, which his followers were expecting almost daily in the period following his crucifixion, and then when this did not occur, continued to be confident that it would at least take place during their own lifetimes. Meher Baba left the mystery of his long silence and his seemingly Unspoken Word.

Chapter 5

TRAVEL IN THE EAST

IT WAS NOVEMBER 1926 when the work at Meherabad was wound up, and almost all buildings apart from Baba's little hut were levelled with the ground. Baba and his followers set off for a neighbouring town in lorries, later travelling on to Bombay by train. But towards the end of December, after an absence of only a few weeks, Baba astonished everyone by ordering a return to the desolate and abandoned Meherabad. Nor was this all; a school was reopened for the village boys, and one soon after for the girls. Later, in April 1927, a school of a new kind was also started. This was a boarding school, known as the Meher Ashram, and it was planned for a special purpose.

Differences of caste and religion have for centuries been the curse of India. They have been a handicap to economic and social development, a cause of smouldering resentment between different peoples, and an obstacle to India's assuming a role of leadership in the modern world. Twenty years after that date, these antagonisms would split the subcontinent, severing Pakistan from India in a violent partition to be followed by massacres, boundary disputes and wars which may even now not be at an end. Politicians and leaders on both sides, despite lofty speeches about unity, have too often either encouraged partisan feelings or allowed themselves to be swept along on a tide of intolerance and hostility.

Boys for the Meher Ashram were chosen from all creeds and classes to receive an education in which spiritual and secular were combined. The aim was to produce a group of educated men, utterly free from prejudice or hostility towards those of different origins, who could serve as a leaven in the life of the community and the world—a parallel today might be the founding of a school in South Africa whose pupils, drawn from all races, would be brought up without trace of colour antagonism. Looking for and accepting the best in one another, the boys would also learn to appreciate the truth in each other's religion and beliefs, so that the way would begin to be paved for acceptance of the universal religion which will one day unite all religions "like beads on a string". The first ten boys to be admitted were four Brahmins (high caste Hindus), three Mahars (untouchables) and three Marathas. These were joined before long by a group from Persia, twelve Zoroastrians and two Moslems. By October 1928, the school had grown to over a hundred, its quarters had been changed several times, and Baba was devoting much time to its organisation and to the boys' spiritual instruction. A tremendous amount of effort had been put into the Meher Ashram and the boys had developed an intense devotional relationship to Baba, and yet some time in 1929 the school was brought to an end. Once again it might appear that a piece of valuable public service had been started, only to be closed abruptly when it might have been expected to achieve most.

It is impossible, however, to form any appreciation of Baba's activities unless one can accept a fundamental fact about his way of working. Baba was never concerned to establish institutions —which inevitably in time become diverted from their original purposes to conform with a general worldly pattern—but rather to accomplish specific parts of his own work. Once the work was done, the 'scaffolding' or organisation was immediately taken down, though in taking it down Baba always made scrupulous provision for all who would be affected by the decision. Why did he not leave the scaffolding up, it may be asked, since even one more school or clinic would be making *some* contribution to the country's social problems? The answer must be that their value depended on the work Baba himself put into them, and that, as soon as his original intention had been achieved, his time and energy had to be put into something else —something which had become at this moment still more urgent.

Every activity Baba undertook was a response to a particular situation he confronted, and until this situation had been met he gave himself to it as whole-heartedly and spontaneously as he gave himself to those who came in contact with him. "I alone do my work," Baba often told his followers, and he alone was the judge of when a particular work had been accomplished. For the mandali, and through them for ourselves, the lesson he conveyed was that the evils of the world are not put right by the founding of institutions, the establishing of societies or the promotion of religious organisations—but only through an immediate loving response to each situation as it arises. This response has to be from person to person and not through institutions, which may indeed serve a temporary purpose and act as a channel for combined effort, but which quickly lose their original impulse and become concerned with their own survival and importance. This is perhaps what Baba meant when he said at Nasik in 1937: "I never make plans, never change plans. It is all one endless plan of making people know that there is no plan."

Meantime from the beginning of 1927, shortly after his return to Meherabad, Baba had ceased to write as well as to speak, and from that time onwards wrote nothing except a rare signature on a photograph or official document.

Though Baba's activity in connection with the Meher Ashram had been intense during the two years, 1927-9, he had also spent periods of up to two months in seclusion and had fasted for as much as five and a half months at a stretch. During this prolonged fast he took nothing except liquids, weak tea, milk or cocoa. 'Fasting' for Baba covered varying degrees of abstinence, from going entirely without food or even water to semi-fasts, in which he took one simple meal every twenty-four hours. Sometimes the mandali, or a few members of it, would be instructed or allowed to share a fast, and sometimes not. Occasionally a fast which had been envisaged did not take place, and once or twice Baba suddenly ordered a special meal to be prepared in haste, of which when the time came he scarcely touched a mouthful.

Baba's explanation of his fasts was simple and surprising. He 'never fasted'. By this he meant that he never went without food in the way saints and yogis do, in order to deny their bodies and increase their spiritual powers. Having no need for such exercises in self-denial, he never refused food when able and inclined to eat it. But the fact was, he explained, that at the times when he fasted he was engaged on spiritual work which rendered it impossible for his physical body to accept food, though the weakness and suffering caused by deprivation were just as acute as any ordinary man would feel. There may be a faint parallel to this in our common experience of inability to eat in times of intense concentration or powerful emotion.

A delightful story in connection with his fasting was told by

Baba many years later at the sahavas (gatherings) in India during November 1955.

> This was also the period when I carried out one of my longest continuous fasts, which lasted five and a half months (November 1927–April 1928). Once during this period I took nothing but a few sips of water for more than twenty-eight days. The remainder of the time I lived on cocoa in milk taken once in twenty-four hours.
>
> Even this was in scant supply as it happened. Lahu [Baba's favourite among the untouchable boys] used to carry my supply to me every day and on the way he would drink half of it and then pass on the other half to me. I found out about this at the end of my seclusion when the women mandali assured me that they had sent Lahu regularly, as I had originally instructed them, with the thermos bottle full of cocoa. When I questioned Lahu about this, he readily confessed pilfering half my cocoa every day. I pardoned the little fellow as readily as he had acknowledged his guilt.*

When not fasting, Baba's diet was sufficiently frugal to constitute the equivalent of a fast by Western standards. He lived mainly on rice and *dal*, a form of vegetable curry. He was vegetarian, though not according to any rigid rule; some of the mandali recalled his having once on an aeroplane journey sent for and eaten a whole tin of spam when this was all that proved to be available. The mandali too were vegetarian, but to his followers in general he allowed freedom to follow their normal way of life. "I allow vegetarians," he said, "to follow their own diet and non-vegetarians to eat meat; I do not interfere with any custom or religion. When faced with love for God these matters have no value." Baba did not touch alcohol, but here too he occasionally overruled his own custom by taking a sip or two of wine and giving it to those about him; he is said once to have been stern with a yogi who refused the drink offered to him in this way. When one of his English followers attending a sahavas asked that a few bottles of whisky be provided in his room, Baba ordered this to be done, and though after the early days of youthful companionship Baba never smoked, he allowed others to smoke freely on social occasions. . . . "When faced with love for God these matters have no value."

* From *Listen Humanity* by D. E. Stevens. Appendix 2.

And now, in April 1929, with the closing of the Meher Ashram, Baba began a period of journeying throughout India with the mandali, as if to prepare them for much greater travels in which before long both he and they were to be involved. During these journeys the party visited cities all over India, Agra, Delhi, Lahore, Quetta, Bombay—partly on foot, and partly by bus and train—also towns with special spiritual associations such as Nasik, Rishikesh and Srinagar. In many of these places large crowds flocked to greet them. From time to time Baba interrupted this life of contact with the people by spells of seclusion and fasting in remote, mountainous places. Near Panchgani in the Western Ghat, where he had been invited by a devotee, Baba arranged for a cave fifteen feet deep to be dug out at a lonely spot near the head of the Tiger Valley, a haunt, as its name implies, of tigers, leopards and other wild creatures. To this cave Baba retired and fasted, a stay which was important, he explained, for his future working. Some of the mandali who were also fasting kept watch from huts above, below and beside the cave to ensure that no strangers came within two hundred yards, no easy task since word of a Master's seclusion in their area brought many people to the spot, some indeed hoping for his blessing, but others out of idle curiosity. They would climb up to the cave in groups of as many as fifty, and the mandali—having of course no legal right, still less the physical power to disperse them—were sometimes hard put to induce them to go home and leave Baba's quiet undisturbed.

After a fortnight spent in this way, Baba summoned the group together one evening at eight o'clock and told them to make ready to leave at once. A bullock cart was found at a small town some miles away and brought up to carry the belongings, and at midnight the party set off on a four-hour descent of the mountains, before returning to Meherabad by bus. Later in the year, after a succession of other journeys, Baba and twelve of the mandali went by bus to Kashmir. Twelve miles north of Srinagar, in a tiny hut at an altitude of about 6,000 feet, Baba again retired into seclusion. Before doing so, however, he allowed all the people from surrounding villages to come and see him; they were mostly poor, and he ordered a feast to be given them.

The hut to which Baba now retired left space for only one man to lie down. Into this he locked himself, and two of the mandali, assisted by a third on night duty, kept watch outside, protected only by the hut's overhanging roof. Baba fasted throughout, taking nothing but water, which was passed to him through an opening at a certain hour daily in response to his knock; fresh water and food for the watchers was carried up twice a day from the village by other members of the mandali. With Baba locked in, the watchers outside, who were forbidden to speak and able to communicate only by signs, found their long vigil frightening. They had a stick to drive away scorpions and snakes, and a fire was kept burning after sunset, but the pitch-dark nights were full of howls and cries, there were sometimes the roar of tigers and the padding of creatures not far off, against which a stick and a fire seemed scant protection. Here too their stay ended without warning, and throughout the entire return journey to Meherabad, lasting for some days, the party took shelter in no resthouse or home. They drove all day from early morning until late at night, stopping in mid-morning when the heat became intense for a meal and a wash, sleeping at night in woods or on the banks of rivers. At the time it must have seemed to some of the followers that much of their hardship was unnecessary, but later when Baba sent them out on long missions and journeys by themselves—in which difficulties and dangers were unavoidable—they looked back thankfully on the arduous training he had given them and the confidence in themselves which they had learned.

And now no sooner was Baba back in Meherabad than he declared he must set off for Persia. He went first to Bombay where word of his arrival brought thousands—Hindus, Moslems, Christians and Parsis—to visit him, and a great crowd assembled to see him off when he left by steamship. The captain and ship's officers were amazed that someone to whom such respect was accorded should be travelling third class with only a seat on a hatch for accommodation, and a wealthy Parsi merchant offered to arrange "a nice cabin in the upper class". Baba's answer was that he was happy where he was, and that "a fakir's place is always with the poorest".

The mandali observed on this tour that though Baba's name was never mentioned and the tour itself kept private, people gathered in every town they came to. In addition there were persons at all levels of life, from government officials and army officers to the humblest workers, with whom some special contact seemed to be made, or perhaps renewed. These experiences started already on the voyage. A member of the engine-room crew, a Moslem, used to come up and stand gazing at him with tears, for minutes at a time. Throughout the five days of the voyage, no word was exchanged, but on the final day Baba beckoned the man over and gave him his handkerchief.

At Bam, a town where Baba put up at a quiet resthouse on the outskirts, several strange incidents happened. A man in imposing military uniform came requesting to see "the Holy Master who has just arrived". Told there was no such person in the resthouse, he persisted that the Holy One be informed that "a beggar has arrived asking for alms from him". Admitted on Baba's instructions, he saluted, laid down his sword, and fell on his knees to kiss Baba's hand. Asked who he was, he replied: "Your humble slave."

"What is your rank?"

"Nothing, beside your Holiness."

"I mean your military rank."

"A General of the Persian army." He later added words strange from the mouth of a high-ranking officer: "I humbly believe that the salvation of this country lies not in its military power but in its spiritual rebirth through an understanding of life, brought about by the benign grace of Great Beings of your exalted dignity, and I humbly pray on behalf of my country for the great gift of your Grace...."

"That is why you see me here," was Baba's acknowledgement and the General withdrew, walking backwards step by step.

In the street just opposite the resthouse was the seat of a saint held locally in high reverence. On Baba's coming out with the mandali for an evening walk, this man rose from his place, and to those who visited him declared that 'the Emperor of all Fakirs' was now present in their midst.

From Persia the party returned to India overland in an eventful journey lasting many days. Back in India Baba made his headquarters for a time at Nasik, a Hindu city of many temples and immense antiquity on the banks of a river 120 miles to the north-east of Bombay. From here and from Meherabad over the next two years, Baba journeyed to South India, twice up to Kashmir in the far north and once again to Persia. At the end of 1930, perhaps as the result of continued travelling in conditions of great hardship, frequently while fasting, Baba's health broke down. It was not long, however, before he recovered to begin an entirely new period of much wider travel.

Chapter 6

TRAVEL IN THE WEST

BABA HAD BEEN warning his followers ever since 1922: "War will break out again, and it will be the worst holocaust the world has ever seen. Almost all the nations will be drawn into it either militarily or economically." And now, in 1931, he started an intensive period of world travel, almost as though intending to make as many visits to the West as possible before the clouds came down. Also, in striking contrast to previous journeys, usually made incognito with strict orders to the mandali not to reveal his name, these visits were publicised and reported. Baba was eager to meet people at all levels; he attended parties, gatherings, theatres; he gave interviews to newspapermen and was photographed for magazines and newsreels.

For his first visit to the West, in September 1931, Baba travelled by sea in the *Rajputana* from Karachi. Nine years before Baba had foretold that on his first trip to the West he would travel with and meet Gandhi, so the mandali were not surprised to learn that the Mahatma was on the same boat, and to receive a message that he would like to come to Baba's cabin for a talk. He had in fact been sent a cable advising him to contact Baba. On his arrival, accompanied by his secretary, Gandhi said he had only come because of the message and could spare no more than five minutes. However he remained for three hours and came back again next day.

"Baba," he said, "it is now time for you to speak and to let the world hear. I feel within me that you are something great: I did not feel the same when I visited Upasni Maharaj."

"Why?" Baba asked.

"When I went to Upasni Maharaj he was wearing a piece of rag around his loins: he removed it and showed his private parts and said "You may be a great man; what is that to me? Why have you come here?""

Baba's reply showed his power to assume authority regardless of whom he was addressing. "Now you really know that I am great, with the authority of that greatness I tell you that Maharaj was a Perfect Master."

But Gandhi was bewildered: "No, Baba, I do not understand it at all." He did, however, return later for a third discussion.

From Europe Baba went on by sea to the United States. Although this was by way of a reconnaissance, paving the way for longer visits, he contacted a great number of men and women, some of whom later became his workers and have remained devoted to him ever since. In March 1932, Baba again set out from India on what was this time virtually a world tour, taking in England, France, Switzerland, the U.S., Honolulu, China, and returning through France, Italy and Egypt. In all, between first leaving the East in the *Rajputana* and October 1937, Baba made no fewer than nine* visits to the West, two of the journeys being 'world tours'. The countries chiefly visited were Britain, America, France, Switzerland and Italy, but he made a fairly long stay also in Spain and went twice to both Egypt and Ceylon.

Baba and his party arrived in London early in April 1932, and Baba gave a number of press interviews. Among those who came to see him was James Douglas, then editor of the *Sunday Express*. Douglas, an able and experienced journalist, had taken a good deal of trouble to prepare himself for the interview.

I had prepared a questionnaire with the help of Sir Denison Ross, the Oriental scholar. It was designed to trap the teacher, but he smilingly threaded his way through it without stumbling. His mastery of dialectic is consummate. It was quite Socratic in its ease.

He frequently put questions to me which startled me by their penetration. But he never evaded a direct question. His simplicity is very subtle.

"I am a Persian," he said. "I was born in Poona, but my father and mother were Persians...."

"Are you divine?" He smiled.

"I am one with God. I live in Him, like Buddha, like Christ, like Krishna. They know Him as I know Him. All men can know Him."

"Have you solved the problem of evil?"

---

* Because on his second journey he came back through Europe from China on his way home to India, some accounts speak of Baba's *ten* visits to the West.

"There is no evil," he said. "There are only degrees of good..."

"What is your secret?" I asked.

"The elimination of the ego," he replied....

"Have you a Scripture, a Bible, a Koran, an inspired book?"

"No, I teach. I am a teacher."*

"Do you believe in Buddha and the Eight-fold Path?"

"Yes. All religion is ascent by stages to perfect union with God."

"What God do you believe in?"

"There is only one God for all men."

"What religion is nearest to yours?"

"All religions are revelations of God."

"Is there a future life?"

"Yes. The soul does not die. It goes on from life to life till it is merged into God."

"Nirvana?"

"Yes. But not loss of the self."

"Does the self survive?"

"Yes. But it is merged in God. The soul is not the brain. It functions in the brain. The brain is its instrument...."

"Is God a Person or a Power?"

"God is both personal and impersonal. He is in art, in literature, everything."

"Are you a Pantheist?"

"No," he smiled. "When you know God it is plain. The Self is one with Him at the height of experience."

"Why am I not happy?"

"You have not grown out of self," he smiled. He had said he would give me a minute, but the minute lasted an hour.

"You are lucky," said a disciple. "He likes you..."

He is serenely certain that he can redeem mankind.

I wonder.†

Not all interviews, however, were as sympathetic as this, or as another which had been published the day before (9th April, 1932) in the *Daily Mirror*. *John Bull* was a weekly magazine founded by Horatio Bottomley, a barn-storming politician of the First World War, and a financial trickster who thrived for

---

* Baba's actual words were: "I awaken."
† Taken from an interview in the *Sunday Express* for 10th April, 1932.

a time in the years which immediately followed. *John Bull*, as its name implied, was a fearless defender of the public, whose safety it ensured by denouncing small-time crooks—absconding Christmas Club secretaries, broken-down clergymen or schoolmasters in trouble—once they had been safely convicted by the courts. It also specialised in "free insurance" schemes to attract readers, to whom it promised compensation for such misfortunes as being struck by lightning, carried away by flood, or losing both arms and legs in a railway accident.

John Bull now published an article in which it declared Baba to be "a fraud". Some of his followers wrote indignantly in his defence, but when Baba heard this he ordered them to stop, first because opposition to him was no fault, and second because: "People who speak ill of me should not be condemned. They, too, are unconsciously serving my work, because they often think of me."

He repeated this in May when he reached New York. His statement ended with the words: "My work will arouse great enthusiasm and a certain amount of opposition*—that is inevitable. But spiritual work is strengthened by opposition, and so it will be with mine. It is like shooting an arrow from a bow—the more you pull the bow-string towards you, the swifter the arrow speeds to its goal."

Baba's visits to London, New York and Chicago had been met with an outburst of publicity which built up to his arrival in Hollywood, described as "a meteoric advent that crashed the front-page headlines of every paper in the land." Hollywood at this time was at its peak, the centre of the first world entertainment industry, as fabulous as Baghdad or Atlantis. Its producers and directors handled budgets larger than those of many countries' exchequers. The influence of its productions was world-wide. Its stars were more famous and admired than kings and queens, more idolised perhaps than any men and women had ever been idolised in history. The 'King' and 'Queen' of Hollywood's court at this time were Douglas Fairbanks and Mary Pickford, who gave a reception in Baba's honour. He spent part of the evening talking to Mary, who was a student of

---

* Another highly critical account of Meher Baba was published in the following year. It is contained in the book *A Search in Secret India* (Rider & Co., 1933) by Paul Brunton, an English journalist whose real name was H. Raphael Hirsch. A second, less antagonistic, is in a book which enjoyed much success, *God is My Adventure*, by Rom Landau (Ivor Nicholson & Watson, 1935).

Eastern philosophy, but also spoke individually to all the other guests. He was received at the principal studios, Fox, Metro-Goldwyn, Warner Brothers, Paramount, and met many of the stars at work. Of the directors, he spent time with Ernst Lubistch and Von Sternberg, then directing Marlene Dietrich in *The Blonde Venus*. Marlene Dietrich was described as off-hand, but Tallulah Bankhead, who returned one evening for a longer interview, became deeply attached to Baba. There are delightful photographs of them together, Baba in an elegant white suit, with flowing hair and open-necked shirt, talking to Tallulah by means of his alphabet board, both entirely concentrated on the interchange. Another with whom he got on happily was Marie Dressler, whose humour delighted him. In the middle of lunch she declared she would like to take Baba out into the woods for a dance, adding that if for once he liked to speak just a few words she would not let anyone know that he had done so.

In all Baba remained six days in Hollywood, which included another evening reception in which he shook hands with a thousand guests as they filed past him. Baba, who was at home with the untouchables at Arangaon or among the travellers camped on a ship's deck in the Indian Ocean, was equally at ease in the luxurious, competitive world of Hollywood. At Pickfair, home of Douglas Fairbanks and Mary Pickford, he gave a message which revealed his knowledge of the cinema and its importance at that time as a medium of communication, and of the inspiration which entertainment, often indirectly, gives to man.

> He who stimulates the imagination of the masses can move them in any direction he chooses, and there is no more powerful instrument for stimulating their imagination than moving pictures.... Both the press and the radio influence thought, but lack the power of visible example which is the greatest stimulant to action, and which the moving pictures offer better now than any other medium...*

Plays which inspire those who see them to greater understanding, truer feeling, better lives, need not necessarily have anything to do with so-called religion. Creed, ritual, dogma, the conventional ideas of heaven and hell and sin, are perversions of the truth, and confuse and bewilder rather than

---

* Noted down by Quentin Tod, who travelled with Baba across America and introduced him to many film people.

clarify and inspire. Real spirituality is best portrayed in stories of pure love, of selfless service, of truth realised and applied to the most humble circumstances of our daily lives, raying out into manifold expression, through home and business, school and college, studio and laboratory . . . producing everywhere a constant symphony of bliss.

This is the highest practicality. To portray such circumstances on the screen will make people realise that the spiritual life is something to be lived, not talked about, and that it—and it alone—will produce the peace and love and harmony which we seek to establish as the constant of our lives.*

Baba had let it be accepted that he would break his silence in the Hollywood Bowl on the 13th July, when a great crowd was expected to gather. But he now said that he must first visit China, and before leaving for Honolulu he sent home his Western followers. Then after two days in Honolulu Baba cabled that he was sailing for Shanghai and would not return to Hollywood. The breaking of a silence which had lasted already for seven years had been much publicised, so the disappointment was correspondingly great. It gave a shock from which not all Baba's Western followers recovered; for many it was their first experience of those abrupt 'changes of plan', familiar to his Eastern followers who had come by now to accept that "there is no plan".

In China, Baba visited Shanghai and Nanking. An English follower, who was at that time a professor at Nanking University, was host to him during his visit. He has left an account in which he stresses, what others frequently noted, Baba's insistence on making contact with people in the mass as well as with individuals.

Baba was dressed in a European suit and a panama hat. I had booked rooms in a hotel overlooking the Bund, the busy street and waterfront of the Whangpoo river.

Immediately we had had tea, Baba said that he wished to go round the city and mix with the Chinese crowds. I had had very little experience of Baba's ways and was still rather

* In London three years later Baba was taken to see Gary Cooper in *Mr Deeds Goes to Town*. He was delighted with the picture, quoting it as an example of the way films can combine entertainment with spiritual truth. Its story, some may remember, is of a battle against corruption in high places.

awkward in his presence. I took them along the Bund, and from the French settlement by tram, through the British to the war-stricken districts near the North station, thinking it would interest them. Not at all. There were not enough people. We took a tram back and saw Nanking Road, the now brightly-lit Chinese Stores, Chungking Road, Racecourse, along Tibet Road. The streets were densely packed with long-gowned clerks and short-coated coolies, endless rickshaw-pullers with cheerful faces and poverty-stricken appearances beseeching us to ride not walk: the narrow streets were hung with paper lanterns and waving banners of Chinese characters. Baba was delighted as we threaded the narrow, perfumed alleys and the Chinese turned to stare at us in a not too friendly manner.

A similar impression was recorded by another companion on Baba's visit to Spain a year later.

He wished to come in contact with the masses. All day we walked along the crowded streets of Madrid until our feet were tired.... Baba particularly loved to stand in the central square, Puerta del Sol, the Gate of the Sun, among the crowds. Every day and several times a day he came here. Sometimes as we walked, despite his normal appearance, European clothes and Spanish beret which concealed his hair, they would turn and stare at him as if drawn by something they could not understand. That night we went to the East End, to a cabaret, a rather low-class dance hall...

Again and again in the cities of the world Baba would insist on being taken to places where many people gathered with their outward attention concentrated, leaving—it would seem—their inner natures free to be contacted by his silent influence. Baba was little concerned what the spectacle might be which attracted the audience's interest, whether *White Horse Inn*, *The Ten Commandments*, a cabaret or a 'low-class dance hall'. Though at times he enjoyed entertainment, particularly if it was funny, he would frequently leave after only a short stay, saying that his work there had been completed.

From Madrid Baba went on to Barcelona, arriving just on the day of celebration for the newly-formed federal state of Catalonia—only too soon to be exterminated when the Spanish Civil War broke out. No one with Baba was aware beforehand of these celebrations which involved a long procession among applauding crowds, but his companions noticed how often Baba's arrival in a place coincided with some important public event resulting in mass gatherings. There was a similar occasion a year later when Baba reached London on the night of a royal wedding, and his party drove past Buckingham Palace and through packed West End streets.

In contrast to the work which Baba accomplished among masses was that which required solitude in a particular setting. Throughout his travels Baba made a point of visiting shrines or holy places connected with great saints or religious figures. Curiosity played no part in this. Caves or shrines in which spiritual work has been accomplished in the past are, it seems, uniquely adapted to such work in the present. In Europe the four most holy places, Baba explained, are at Assisi, Avila, St Mark's in Venice, and a spot on the Ligurian coast, and in each of these he spent a period of time, though this was sometimes difficult to arrange. He also visited sacred places in Egypt and Ceylon.

The Coptic church in Cairo contains, he said, a cave where Joseph and Mary with the infant Jesus rested on the flight from Herod. His objective in Ceylon was a Buddhist temple up in the hills at a place called Bandravella. Here, as at Assisi, Baba wanted to retire for twenty hours into seclusion at the chosen spot without risk of interruption. No progress in the negotiations was being made until an aged man appeared who seemed to recognise Baba, communicated with him by signs, and then ordered a room to be made ready in which he could remain undisturbed.

Chapter 7

BRINGING EAST AND WEST TOGETHER

THROUGHOUT HIS LIFE, almost indeed from his schooldays, Baba had emphasised with words and action the need to bring East and West together. To bring together individual Easterners and Westerners had been one of the purposes of his period of world travel, and again and again in prepared statements and informal talks he stressed the need for a union between their two attitudes of mind. On his first arrival in New York he had given a message in which he said:

> I have come to help people realise their ideals in daily life.... My work and aims are intensely practical. It is not practical to emphasise the material at the cost of the spiritual. It is not practical to have spiritual ideals without putting them into practice. But to realise the ideal in daily life, to give beautiful and adequate form to the living spirit, to make Brotherhood a fact, not merely a theory, as at present—this is being practical in the truest sense of the word.

Five years earlier, in establishing the Meher Ashram, Baba had made efforts to include some English pupils, sending a special representative over to Britain to arrange this. Though this particular project did not materialise, numbers of Westerners had at different times come over to stay at Meherabad and other places serving as his headquarters. For his journeys to the West Baba took with him members of the mandali who besides making personal contacts also became familiar with Western attitudes to life, experiencing at first hand that energetic handling of practical problems and material difficulties which Baba so often praised. But it was not only in work that Baba brought the two worlds together. More than once while in Europe he took combined parties of Westerners and Easterners to stay with him for some weeks in holiday surroundings. There was such a stay at Santa Margherita in Italy during August 1932, of which one of the women kept the following account.

> These Italian days with Baba were very happy times. Warm sun, blue sea, a wonderful coastline, and behind the hotel green hills and shaded walks through vineyards and forests. In the morning we trooped down to the rocks, bathed, dived, splashed or basked in the sun, Baba in our midst...
>
> Baba's room led out on to a private balcony. When we swam before breakfast we could see his white-clad figure watching us from the balcony. Often at night we would sit there listening to music on the gramophone: Baba's favourites were Indian and Persian spiritual songs which he would explain to us, Spanish dances and Paul Robeson's negro spirituals. On the terrace we would act charades or get up entertainments. Under the name of Thomas, Baba would also take dancing lessons from one of us who was a skilled dancing instructor. Thus, and in innumerable ways, Baba entered into our lives as playmate, friend, child and father...

In the following year, 1933, Baba took a similar party to stay at Portofino, where again their visit was a blend of holiday enjoyment with spiritual training, and there was a further party on similar lines at Cannes in 1937. Meantime, earlier in 1933, he had taken another step towards co-ordination by arranging for a party of Western women to visit India. It was one thing for them to meet the men of the mandali, widely travelled and accustomed by now to Western ways, and another to get to know the Indian women living what was at that time their extremely secluded life. In the event contacts were few and the party went home earlier than had been expected. A start had been made, however, and three years after this, in October 1936, Baba visited London, Zurich and Paris in the company of only two disciples. His purpose was to arrange for followers from England and America, including both women and men, to join the new ashram he had established in the ancient and holy city of Nasik. "I want them with me because the time is at hand for me to do much work, and I want them to share my work."

And so by Christmas 1936, six women and two men from the U.S., with four women and two men from Britain, were established in a comfortable house outside Nasik. All had given two promises: to live together harmoniously, and to remain for five years. Nasik was only a few hours by car from Meherabad, the home of the women mandali, and every two weeks the Western women were taken over for a visit, of which Jean Adriel, author of the book *Avatar*, set down her impressions.

Their 'House on the Hill', in which they lived their quiet, gentle lives, was surrounded by a wall twelve feet high. This enclosed a compound of about forty square feet upon which two houses faced. The larger one consisted—at that time—of a single room about thirty feet by twenty. The chief appointments of the room were six iron beds, each with its mosquito-netting canopy. Beside each bed was a small wooden trunk, in which were kept the few belongings of the women, and a straight wooden chair. There were no ornaments, no gadgets, no books. The most austere convent would be luxurious by comparison. . . . Though on the surface their lives were acutely circumscribed, monotonous and meagre, their faces bore the unmistakable imprint of a happier, more contented life than we Westerners with our so-called full, colourful lives had ever known. . . . Having no need to disburden themselves of mental impressions, and feeling no inclination towards gossip, they spoke but little. But one could see that they lived deeply, consciously, each one a distinct *individual*.

Among the six who formed the women mandali at that time were two uniquely close to Baba, both of whom would become well known in later years to his followers throughout the world. One of these was his sister Mani, described by Jean Adriel at this time as "a beautiful young woman about eighteen . . . very versatile in her creative gifts. She writes, paints, sings, dances and acts with charming spontaneity and grace." Mani, who acted as a secretary to Baba, wrote the 'Family Letters' sent out regularly every few months from 1956-69 to keep Westerners in touch at a time when Baba was spending long periods in seclusion. The other was Mehera (Mehera J. Irani), Baba's chief woman disciple; 'The Beloved's Beloved', a beautiful, stately and gentle woman. While still a young girl, she with her mother, Daulatmai, had been among the first to join the ashram at Meherabad when women were allowed to do so. Since then her life has been one of entire devotion to Baba, passed mainly in strict seclusion, though she also accompanied Baba on some of his travels inside India, and two or three times to Europe and America.

To these women, whose furthest journey at that time had only been from one ashram to another, the arrival of the visitors must have been an experience just as disturbing as it was for the Westerners to find themselves among women who lived in a manner and by values so different from their own. "In the Western group," Jean Adriel records,* "was a former dancer in the Russian ballet (Margaret Craske); a woman with her own insurance business in New York (Elizabeth Patterson); an actress who had held salons in many of the large European cities (Norina Matchabelli); two other actresses (Delia de Leon and Ruano Bogislav); an artist (Rano Gayley); and one who had devoted a number of years to social work in the slums, alms-houses, prisons and hospitals of New York, Philadelphia and Pittsburgh (Jean Adriel). Practically all were women who had travelled extensively and seen much of what is popularly termed 'life'."

Despite their background of sophistication, it was the Western women who felt overawed by these meetings. "Because we Westerners were still far from the conscious inner freedom which these holy women enjoyed, many of us suffered acutely on the Meherabad trips. I felt as if I were being required to function in a kind of mental vacuum. . . . It was like being dropped into a fair country where language is neither spoken nor read, but where people go about their affairs with serene, happy faces, communicating with each other by some inner means which one does not yet know."

Baba had warned the Western visitors: "As part of your training you will have to experience both the comforts of Nasik and the discomforts of Meherabad." Later he explained: "I want you to lead a simple life here in India; then, when you return to the West you may resume your accustomed life there, yet you must be unaffected by either. In view of this you may wonder why I have arranged these comforts for you. If I required you to sleep on the floor, for example, the body would rebel and in turn react upon the mind. Such sudden, drastic changes would make it difficult for me to impart truth to you through the mind. I will therefore gradually withdraw these comforts from you and later return them to you again. The world is slave to needs. The needs must become your slaves. You

* *Avatar*, p. 188.

must learn to use your modern conveniences—not be used by them."

The intention had been that, after three months in Nasik, the Western women should take part in the austere life of Meherabad, but in fact they remained the whole time in Nasik. Here disagreements and upsets arose, until finally a crisis developed in the group, and by the end of July most were sent home. Later the same year, however, following the holiday in Cannes, three Western women returned with Baba's party to India, to be joined later on by three others who had gone home first to see their families. And now the shared life of the two groups really began. A second story had been added to the 'House on the Hill', forming a dormitory with cubicles separated by curtains, corresponding to the large room shared by the women mandali below. All the women were given arduous tasks to perform, partly in the running of a women's hospital which had been opened.

When the inevitable conflicts and even quarrels arose, Baba did not seek to damp them down. On the contrary, he would allow them to develop and then call those involved together and face them with the situation, often compelling them to speak out and say what they thought of one another. Only then, when everything had been brought out into the open, would he resolve the conflict. "If you cannot love each other, then learn to give in," he told them, and in the course of giving in they found they did come to love each other. Some of them still share a common life and a common devotion nearly forty years later.

What must we suppose to have been the purpose behind these persistent efforts to unite two groups of women who in upbringing and outlook were at first such poles apart? Did Baba give so freely of his time and energy in order that some half-dozen Western women should learn a deeper outlook on the world, and that an equal number of the East—albeit those closest to him—should assimilate the experience, and develop that capacity to cope with the material world, which distinguishes the West?

It was Baba's way, and is said to be the practice of all Perfect Masters, to work out in their lifetimes on a small scale models for developments which will later become world-wide. Throughout his life Baba constantly emphasised the importance of woman and the values particularly associated with her, love, tenderness, service to others, stressing them not as something to be demanded of woman by man for his enjoyment or advantage, but as qualities he must value in her and develop in himself. So in bringing the groups together with such patience and determination, Baba was perhaps—for all attempts to interpret are only guesswork—achieving three aims at the same time, among perhaps many others. He was sowing the seeds of a unity between East and West. He was stressing the importance of woman for the coming age; and he was helping to develop a pattern of what kind of woman she would be—one in whom the talent, the energy and practical capacity of the Westerners would be blended with the devotion and spirituality of the women mandali.

Woman has to be liberated, not in order to become man's imitation or enslaver, but to become something new, something more than she has ever been till now—and in so doing to inspire man to become more than he has ever thought of being, more than he has ever been willing to become. Her role, following that of Baba himself, is to awaken.

Chapter 8

THE 'GOD-INTOXICATED' (1)

SIX YEARS HAD been spent by Baba in forging links with the West. At times his world tours wore almost the aspect of social visits. Film-stars, writers, musicians, artists, bankers, businessmen, politicians—Baba had been happy to meet everyone and had time for everyone. His engagements might have been, and sometimes were, chronicled in newspapers and gossip columns. But now, for a period extending over nearly thirteen years, he focused his attention upon a group of beings unknown outside their own localities, virtually inaccessible to normal contact, and only contactable by Baba himself at immense cost in physical and inner effort. And, incidentally, at great financial cost as well. "Money came to me in waves," he remarked in 1954, "and as waves it rolled away." One of the waves which rolled away was the cost of searching out and caring for the 'God-mad' or 'God-intoxicated'.

To the Western mind this aspect of Baba's work is at the same time fascinating and perplexing. It also appears to be unique, having no parallel in the life of any other spiritual Master. But its importance is shown, first, by the fact that Baba devoted to it more than one-sixth of his whole life, and, secondly, by the period at which this activity was taking place. For these years, 1936–49, coincided with the approach, onset, duration and aftermath of the Second World War, the supreme crisis for both Eastern and Western worlds. They culminated in the dropping of the atomic bomb, the establishment of the 'Iron Curtain', and the tension over the Berlin Blockade, which was within an inch of leading to war between the Western powers and the U.S.S.R.: and they included the Chinese revolution, the achievement of Indian independence after centuries of foreign domination, with the tragic migrations and slaughter of refugees consequent upon partition.

So that throughout those years, when the sane and practical peoples of the world were almost entirely occupied with the madness and waste of war, Baba was concentrating his efforts and resources upon a few hundred persons whom these same practical peoples would consider to be mad. Today, thirty years later, Baba's work with the God-mad may seem a little less strange, for in an age when all barriers are collapsing and classifications dissolving into one another, the distinction between 'mad' and 'sane' is dissolving too, so that the more aware any of us become of our own natures, the more reluctant we are to claim sanity or impute madness.

As was often his way, Baba found his own word for the God-mad; he called them 'masts'.* Of his work among the masts, and of the strange individualities of the masts themselves, a record happily exists. It was compiled, surprisingly, by a Westerner, Dr William Donkin, who in 1938 had given up his career in England, his family and country, in order to be with Baba, as he said, "till the end". Baba many times suggested that he was free to return to England if he wished, but he always insisted on remaining. He was one of very few Westerners who ever formed part of the mandali, and the only one to belong to it throughout this period and during the succeeding period of the 'New Life'. What makes Dr Donkin's book *The Wayfarers*† so overpowering is partly the nature of its subject matter, and partly the fact that the author was at the same time doctor and writer. He had the interest to study and sympathy to penetrate the confusion in which the masts, like the mad, are shrouded, and the capacity to express what he saw and understood. His little-known book, from which virtually everything in this and the following chapter has been taken, is one of those unknown in their own age, but to which new stages in man's development are certain one day to bring appreciation and acclaim.

What is a mast, and how is a mast distinguished from a common madman?

Masts are of many types—actually, Baba said, of no fewer then fifty-six—and he explained to his followers some of their distinguishing characteristics and stages of development. But there is one characteristic shared by all. They are dead to the

* Mast, pronounced 'must', may be derived from a Sufi expression, or else from a Persian word meaning 'overpowered'. However, the use Baba made of it was his own.
† *The Wayfarers* by William Donkin, with a foreword by Meher Baba. Published 1948, by Adi K. Irani, Kings Rd, Ahmednagar, for Meher Publications. Dr Donkin died in August 1969, little more than six months after Baba himself.

world and living inwardly in bliss, to which the nearest parallel most of us can imagine would be the early stages of happy intoxication. But for the mast this state is permanent. The mast, in Baba's words, "... lives and knows only God. He loses all consciousness of self, of body and the world. Whether it rains or shines, whether it is winter or summer, it is all the same to him. He is dead to himself."

And of a particular mast, he said: "He has no body consciousness. He remains in the same position for hours together without moving his limbs in the slightest degree... He is not mad, but looks like it. He is also childlike. If you make him stand up, he will remain standing until you tell him to sit down again.* His mind does not function as the mind of an ordinary human being; yet his mind is not blank. Intense love and longing for God has made him like dust. This mast does not belong to the world, though he is in it."

To be in the world, yet not belong to it or be dominated by it, has been stated by every religion as a principal aim of man's life on earth, and the mast has achieved this condition. But he has achieved it at the cost of losing his awareness of external reality and even of his own body and its functions. To the outward eye therefore the mast is only a madman, a fragment in that tide of derelicts who drift up and down the Indian sub-continent or squat stranded by its dusty roadsides. In the West we have no tradition and no conception, not even any myths or fairy-tales, concerned with the God-mad—and no wonder, for in our society no creatures of the sort exist. They are as remote as coelacanths, or fishes from the utmost depths, to paddlers on seaside beaches. We Westerners do indeed 'go out of our minds'. We 'become beside ourselves' with the strain of competition, through fear of deprivation or of failure. But we do not go out of our minds through love of God. In India, however, spirituality is a most powerful preoccupation and great numbers of men, women, children even, apply themselves to spiritual development with the passionate determination which we give to making money, following sport, gratifying desire, or trying to alter the world and other people through political action.

Though we have no conception of the 'God-mad' or 'God-intoxicated'—and indeed a 'God-intoxicated' clergyman could hardly expect to remain long in office—we do have the ex-

---

* cf. p. 26. The condition Baba himself was in after his initiation by Babajan.

pression 'divine madness', and we recognise certain exceptions, or half-exceptions, to the materialistic order. Artists, musicians, writers are expected to show eccentricity of behaviour and indifference to money values, the willingness to starve in garrets, enduring a lifetime of deprivation in the hope perhaps of posthumous recognition. Philosophers and thinkers, we consider, should be unworldly, forgetful of everyday requirements, inwardly absorbed. The eccentric artist and the absent-minded professor are perhaps our nearest equivalent to the God-mad. And the familiar lines of Dryden—

> Great wits are sure to madness near alli'd,
> And thin partitions do their bounds divide—

would never have been so popular as to be regularly misquoted if they were not held to contain an important truth.

Throughout the Moslem world, however, madness is commonly associated with spiritual development and what may be a blinding awareness of God's presence. Madmen are seldom confined. They are treated with tolerance, almost reverence, and it is a religious duty to contribute to their needs. Masts are frequently Moslem by religion, though there are also many Hindus. They are found, Baba explained, almost entirely in India, though there are a few also in Egypt and Arabia, and a very few in Iran and Tibet. There are none at all in Europe and the Americas, though there are saints, mystics and devout followers of God. It is India's pervasive climate of spirituality which accounts for the flowering of so many of the God-mad, who themselves in turn intensify that climate.

There are, of course, many false masts and sham sadhus. Baba himself in the course of his search for masts and advanced souls visited Allahabad in February 1948 for a great fair which is held only every six years, to which thousands of sadhus come together from all over India to bathe at the confluence of two sacred rivers, the Jumna and the Ganges. At this fair, among something like a million persons, there were estimated to be 30,000 sadhus. The estimate is more than a guess, since sadhus of many sects attend and each sect has its own territory reserved for it. In the course of a morning, Baba went around all the territories, contacting some 4,000 sadhus. He afterwards told the mandali that among these four thousand there were no more than seven advanced souls.

However, the fact that among many so-called 'holy men' the

vast majority are less than holy, does not affect the picture of India in general. There are in the capitalist West many dishonest financiers and incompetent industrialists, but in financial and industrial development the West nonetheless leads the world. Similarly in Communist countries there are many high officials whose main interest is private gain, but the preoccupation of these countries as a whole is with political development on Socialist lines. It is not the honesty or otherwise of individuals which creates a climate, but the concentration of interest in the minds of ordinary people, and in India that concentration is on spiritual things.

A remarkable example of this was shown in Madras over a mast named Mohammed Mastan. Two members of the mandali had come upon him in a back street, and were concerned that Baba should have the opportunity of sitting with him in seclusion. The only place which offered privacy was the office of a small private bank, into which the two followers went and put forward the request on their master's behalf. Without question or argument, the banker ordered his clerks into the street and himself followed them out, leaving his office littered with money and papers, so that Baba should be able to sit there with the mast for a short while undisturbed.

Apart from being constantly in a state of God-intoxication, what are the other characteristics of a mast? One Westerners have difficulty in accepting is that they are frequently found in sordid surroundings, in a state of personal neglect, and even filth. Baba, who devoted hours each day for months on end to washing and bathing masts, has explained their condition.

> From general standards of society, religion, health, morality and so forth, cleanliness of body and mind are indispensable. It is, however, very easy to keep the body clean; but cleanliness of mind is very difficult indeed. The more one gets attached to body cleanliness for merely selfish reasons, the less are the chances of having a clean mind.
>
> If, however, one is given up wholly to mental cleanliness, which means becoming free from low, selfish, impure desires and thoughts of lust, greed, anger, backbiting etc., the less is one's mind attached to bodily needs and bodily cleanliness. . . .
>
> You will find that the majority of ordinary mad people have very little consciousness of their bodies. So if an ordinary

mind, when mad, does not pay attention to bodily cleanliness, then ... (masts) who unconsciously or consciously know all the universe to be zero, body to be a shadow, and whose minds are absolutely unattached to the body, cannot be expected to keep their bodies and surroundings clean. ...

For these souls, good or bad, cleanliness or dirt, a palace or a hut, a spotless avenue or a filthy gutter are all the same, and they are driven into any of these places according to circumstances.

However dirty the mast may be, and however scanty or unsuitable his diet, he remains physically healthy, resistant to exposure and extremes of climate far beyond the endurance of normal men, and frequently lives to a great age. Of one such Baba said: "Divine love is the fire which not only eliminates all kinds of cold, but all sorts of imagined heat. For example, amongst the very, very few who possess such love is the mast known as Dhondipa at Kolhapur. Though exposed to the rigours of heat, cold and rain through all the seasons, his body remains healthy, well-fleshed and strong. The fire is burning within him unknown to those in his surroundings. His mind has no link with his body. Love pervades him from head to foot."*

Another mast who possessed this resistance to an eminent degree was Chatti Baba, a prince among masts, who remained for two years with Baba. Dr Donkin writes of him: "In Quetta, where the weather was still colder, he used to pour icy water on his bedding, and sit on it. One day, there was such a monstrous hailstorm that the hailstones took three or four days to melt, and on the night following the storm, Chatti Baba sat stripped to the waist on the hail from four until seven in the morning."

A violent temper† is characteristic of many masts, or its opposite, extreme passivity. Common to many is also a childlike capriciousness. They will ask for something and on receiving it immediately hand it back or give it away. In their detachment from all worldly values, their restless fancy lights upon chance objects, rags, old papers, pieces of rubbish, which they collect

---

* *Meher Baba on Love*, compiled by Shri K. K. Ramakrishnan, published by Meher Era Publication, Poona. It was this same mast who, when offered anything for his material needs, would refuse it, saying: "I cannot bear comfort."

† This is not due to personal antagonism, but arises from a fierce resistance to any interruption of the mast's inner bliss. Passivity is another way of avoiding such interruption.

and hoard—or else give away. Baba, who kept no possessions, treasured the 'worthless' objects given to him by masts. All these and similar eccentricities may be equally typical of ordinary madmen, and Dr Donkin records that—with all the expertise which certain members of the mandali developed in the recognition and handling of masts—they made mistakes and brought along persons of little or no spiritual development. So that in the last resort a man was accepted as a mast because Baba said he was one. Dr Donkin adds, however, two interesting perceptions of his own, first that, "however strangely they (masts) may behave, they make one feel unmistakably happy in their company. They do not exhale any of that subtle antipathy that seems to emanate from the insane, but actually kindle a sense of harmony in one's self." His second observation is that animals are attracted to masts and masts to them, and he records instances of masts whose abodes were shared by a pack of stray dogs, cats or other animals, adding that such masts invariably feed their animals before taking anything themselves.

Masts live in literal accord with the instruction of Jesus to "take no thought for the morrow": indeed they take no thought for today. Yet there is always someone to feed them and care for them to the degree they will allow. Sometimes this is a personal attendant or disciple, drawn by devotion, respect, or the hope of spiritual progress. Sometimes it is a relative who assumes the task as a duty, and Dr Donkin records the extraordinary case of a Bombay family in which two brothers were masts and seven sisters mastanis (female masts), all nine being looked after by their eldest brother who alone was leading a conventional life. Sometimes a group will adopt a mast as a kind of patron saint. The great mast Ali Shah of Ahmednagar was so adopted by a group of bus drivers, men who—in India as elsewhere—are of a type little given to sentimental gestures. People in well-to-do circumstances—civil servants, station masters, senior clerks—sometimes allow a mast to settle on the verandah of their bungalow, and see that his modest needs are met, much as some Western businessmen or their wives support a favourite charity. This can make heavy demands on a host's goodwill, as Dr Donkin records in the case of Aghori Baba of Simla.

> A very high mast.... He is a very impressive and powerful-looking man with fiery eyes, and he sits covered only with a piece of sack on the verandah.... All about him he has

collected piles of rubbish and rags, and the owner of the house —a Sikh—is now unable to enter his house by way of his own verandah, for not only is it chock-a-block with the rags and rubbish belonging to Aghori Baba, but also if he ventures to enter by this route, the mast rebuffs him with abuse. The Sikh, therefore, has set up a ladder by means of which he bridges over the territory upon which Aghori Baba dislikes him to trespass, and so reaches his house.

Baba has summed up for us the difference between a God-mad and a lunatic in a couple of sentences. To the outward eye both seem alike; the difference is within. "The mind of an ordinary madman has failed to adapt itself to the problems of the material world, and has fled permanently into the realm of make-believe to escape an intolerable material situation. But a God-mad man, though he has lost the balance of his mind and the insight into his abnormal state, has not come to this condition by failing to solve his worldly troubles, but has lost his sanity through continually thinking about God."

Unlike the madman, therefore, who is in a state of confusion, anger and despair, the mast is in a state of unalloyed, intoxicated bliss.

Chapter 9

THE 'GOD-INTOXICATED' (2)

BABA'S WORK AMONG masts was carried on in two ways, both means to the same end. In one, groups of masts were concentrated in ashrams or communal dwelling-places temporarily established at convenient spots, where Baba with the help of the mandali tended and took care of them. Mast ashrams in six centres* strategically placed all over India occupied much of Baba's time and attention from August 1936 to October 1940. Some years later two more ashrams were established for brief periods, December 1946–January 1947 and June–July 1947. The six years in between, roughly from 1941–6, were the years of the great 'mast tours' in which Baba ranged from end to end of the sub-continent seeking out and contacting advanced souls. In all he travelled no less than 75,000 miles, from Ceylon up to the Himalayas, from Bombay in the west to Calcutta in the east, with innumerable shorter journeys. He was in every province except Assam, in every great city and many smaller ones, as well as in hundreds of remote villages—making, his followers reckoned, some 20,000 contacts in his search for masts and spiritual pilgrims.

Mast ashrams were accommodated in houses or bungalows let or temporarily rented. Usually these included outhouses or servants' quarters which could be adapted to provide the simple accommodation the masts preferred. For Baba there was either a cottage or hut, or else one would be constructed in which he could sit in private with each mast. An odd addition to the Bangalore ashram was a 'mast hotel'. Masts enjoy frequenting tumbledown teashops, so to make them feel at home one was "constructed with diligent negligence, everything a trifle awry, with low roof, crooked pillars, and limping tables and chairs".

---

* They were at Rahuri, Ajmer, Jubbulpore, Bangalore, Meherabad and Ranchi, and a glance at the map will show that they were indeed 'strategically placed'. The two later ashrams were at Mahabaleshwar and Satara, both of them close to the Meherabad headquarters.

THE 'GOD-INTOXICATED' (2)

Here they were served with tea, cigarettes, beedies (locally-made cigarettes of the cheapest kind, looking more like matchsticks than cigarettes), or p̂an* as often as they asked, for Baba made it a rule that the masts were to be given at once whatever they wanted.

Since masts are absorbed in inner contemplation, it is painful for them to be brought sharply down to earth as can be done when their wishes are crossed. Masts would sometimes fly into rages or, if of the submissive type, burst into tears over seeming trifles, and it was to avoid such distresses that Baba gave orders for their wishes to be indulged. How far he would go himself to meet a mast's demands was shown in the case of Moienuddin of Hyderabad, for whom Baba had to wait three hours before he allowed himself to be fed. When finally Baba had succeeded in feeding a substantial meal to him, Moienuddin called for mincemeat, then for a chapatti, tea, sweetmeats—and lastly for a special kind of bread hard to obtain. All were brought him and, when every whim had been satisfied, Moienuddin agreed to co-operate.

When a new mast was brought into the ashram, a first task was to bathe and shave him, which Baba did himself. Bathing for some was a simple matter, but other masts would refuse point-blank, and have to be coaxed, gently but persistently, into consenting; others were in such a state of neglect that a first bath lasted hours. After a while some masts began to take pleasure in the bath and insist on prolonging the enjoyment; one of the greatest, Chatti Baba, used to call for 150–200 buckets of water, and would sit "chuckling and gurgling happily" while all this was poured over him. Once bathed, the incoming mast was given clean clothing and then fed by Baba, usually by hand as one feeds a small child. In addition each mast was given a coin. Since embarking on his silence, Baba never touched money, but he made an exception for the masts. The gift was not charity so its value was unimportant. What mattered, Baba explained, was that, being metal, the coin served as a medium of contact.† Only

---

* P̂an, familiar on the trays or baskets of Indian roadside sellers, is a bright green leaf, which is dexterously folded and secured with a clove as pin. Inside are spices. The whole little bundle is put into the mouth and chewed. One result is a scarlet saliva which stains gums and lips, and often dribbles in rivulets from the corners of an addict's mouth.

† It is said that an initiate into Freemasonry has to have all metal removed from his person. Special clothing is worn in which tapes are used to avoid having metal fasteners.

when all this had been accomplished would Baba sit with the mast in silent conference.

These conferences afforded the spiritual contact to which everything else led up. They might take place by day or night, at any hour, but always in secret, consequently no eyewitness account of what took place exists. Dr Donkin records, however, that when Baba was working with a high mast who co-operated fully, the effort and drain on his vitality were immense, so that he would emerge from a session "pale, and apparently exhausted, his clothes often drenched in perspiration out of all proportion to the heat of the day". Nothing made him so happy, however, as a successful session with such a one as Chacha of Ajmer, of whom Baba said that he was "'as good as a hundred ordinary masts". Working with Chacha he would become so engrossed as utterly to forget meals, sleep, the mandali—"and, it seems, the whole wide world". And Dr Donkin gives this glimpse of Baba in February 1940, as he saw him in an interval of his mast work:

> He was looking radiantly noble with hair let down for once. . . . His phenomenal strength of character and sort of mysterious spiritual beauty were astonishing as he sat on his couch. Baba's face in repose has a fusion of spiritual bliss and serenity yet such sadness which gives it grandeur. His face really surpasses all experience of nature in its hold on the beholder, and in its rapid changes of mood.

No doubt the main reason for Baba's insistence on absolute seclusion during his sessions with the masts lay in the nature of his spiritual work. But Dr Donkin suggests as a secondary reason the physical danger, both to the mast and to any intruder upon spiritual proceedings at this level, and he instances the experience of Eruch—Baba's 'right hand'—who once, after Baba had been closeted with Chatti Baba for about two hours, heard sounds of movement and went forward to release a door catch. Chatti Baba, emerging from the session, brushed past him, causing "a palpable and excruciating shock" which made Eruch feel as though he were being electrocuted.

Whenever an ashram closed because work in that area had been completed, great care was taken to ensure the well-being of all masts. Usually they were happy to return to their own town or village, and the people would eagerly welcome back their 'patron saint'. The mast would be given a parting gift of blanket or clothing, and a member of the mandali would escort him home. Where necessary a sum of money would be handed over to someone in his neighbourhood to look after him and feed him twice a day. Only when all such arrangements had been completed would the party set out for its next objective. Usually the journey was by bus, its roof piled high with bedding rolls, cooking pots, baths—all the gear and impedimenta of perhaps thirty people. One particular journey half up the Indian continent from Bangalore to Meherabad was made by rail, and gives a glimpse of what such journeys could be like.

The mandali, twenty odd madmen, five or six masts, a gazelle, a peacock, a sheep, a white rabbit, some geese, five dogs, three monkeys, and two pet birds were all crammed into this one compartment* and sat cheek by jowl with the trunks, packing cases, tables, chairs, and the inevitable medley of domestic and culinary equipment.... As soon as the train started, Shariat Khan—one of the masts—tied bells to his ankles, and danced to a rhythm beaten out by Punjia on his kerosene tin. Punjia danced as he drummed, and made Eruch and Baidul join in. Once or twice stray strangers tried to get in, but changed their minds after one glance through the window.

The work on mast tours was partly contacting masts for the future, and partly similar to that done in the ashrams, but far more pressurised and exhausting since it was carried out on the move. In everything he did or that was done for him, Baba insisted on the most careful planning. "I have that bad Avataric habit," he once said, "of supervising every detail myself," so every tour was precisely planned, and preceded by a preliminary survey in which two or three members of the mandali would be sent over the ground beforehand, meeting and observing likely souls. Such reconnoitring expeditions were made always under pressure, at minimal expense, and often in extreme discomfort from heat, floods, and the difficulties of travel in remote parts of the country. The three most experienced 'mast discoverers' were considered to be Baidul, Eruch and Kaka, and they spoke feelingly of "tramping on foot across arid sands, through dark forests, or over mountain and valley: of riding on camels, mules, ponies and asses; of bumping over mile after mile of purgatorial

---

* It must surely have been a whole railway coach, not what we understand by a 'compartment'.

tracks in bullock carts and tongas; of enduring nights and days in the dusty and sweaty turmoil of overcrowded third class railway carriages... in the mere preliminary reconnaissance of almost every one of Baba's mast tours".

These hardships, however, were insignificant compared with those accepted as a matter of course on the tours themselves. Here Baba set the pace and—like that at which he often walked—it was one which tested his and their endurance to the utmost. "After two or three days of work from dawn to dusk with little or no food, and after two or three nights with little or no sleep," Dr Donkin records, "the world simply becomes unreal, and one lives a kind of reflex life in which the parts of one's body move and work; but the zest of living, and that sense of well-being, dependent one supposes, upon a nervous system refreshed by sleep, and upon tissues nourished by adequate food, are simply no longer there. But mast tours do not last just two or three days, they go on for two or three weeks, and this tempo of work goes on and on, Baba ever spurring those with him to the very limits of their powers. On one of the tours in 1946, Baidul estimated that, in eight days, they had a *total* of fourteen hours' sleep.... Finally, add to all these things the infliction of a tropical climate, and the drain on one's vitality through constant perspiration, and you will get an approximate answer of what a mast tour is like."

On one tour when the party dossed down on a railway platform, they were so exhausted that a petty thief crept in and shared Baba's blanket unnoticed by anyone. Questioned in the morning, he admitted to being a thief but said he had only come there for shelter, and Baba told the mandali to let him go.

Besides the hardships of travel, there were endless problems with the masts themselves. The fact that a mast had been approached by one of the mandali was no guarantee that he would still be in the same place, or in the mood to come forward when required. Sometimes a mast had disappeared; some made difficulties over being brought to Baba, as if sensing they would be called on for some profound effort or sacrifice. At times their reaction on meeting Baba was ambivalent, as if in self-protection. Bhayya Baba of Kishangarh was first met with in an eating house. Asked to sit near Baba, he objected: "I know what your work with me is, and I won't come." When Baba wanted to feed him, he said shrewdly: "Give me food, I will eat it myself here." However, with persistence and persuasion—and it must be remembered that Baba himself could never speak—Bhayya Baba at last gave his co-operation.

In the approaches to masts Baba never allowed his name to be disclosed. Masts had to come of their own free will to meet 'the Master', or at least with reluctant consent, not impelled by the authority of his name. How powerful this authority was for them emerged in their talk. In the ashram at Ajmer, the attendant whose special task it was to look after Chatti Baba became so exasperated one day that he felt like walking out. "You want to leave, don't you?" the great mast rebuked him. "But what's the good of it? All the world's in Baba's power, so where will you go to? Serve him now, he is the ocean, because one day when lots of people throng to see him, you may never get the opportunity...."

The same metaphor was used by other masts. Khala Masi, a woman mast, said to Baba: "You are the Ocean. Give me a few drops from it to drink." Another, refusing to come, gave as his excuse: "My boat will be drowned in that Ocean." Pir Fazl Shah, a pilgrim, spoke of a flood: "No one until you came has touched my heart with the arrow of Divine Love. You have the power to destroy and flood the whole world. No one fully knows the limits of your greatness: You are the spiritual authority of the time and if I were to die I would take another body to be close to you." Another mast being brought to Baba said, on reaching the gate: "We have come to the garden of Paradise." When Baba came out, he gazed at him, laughing with tears of joy, and then embraced him. "Look at this man's face and forehead!" he exclaimed to those about him, "They shine as if the sun were there. Can't you recognise who he is?"

What was the purpose of Baba's work among masts? It would seem to have been partly for humanity at large, and partly for the masts themselves. Dr Donkin says in the foreword to his book:

> Because of his being stationed on the inner planes, which are free from the limitations and handicaps of the gross world, a mast can be, and often is, in contact with a far greater number of souls than is possible for an ordinary person.... A mast can therefore be a more effective agent for spiritual work than the most able persons of the gross world. The mast mind is also

often used directly by the Master as a medium for sending his spiritual help to different parts of the world. Very often, when the Master is helping a mast, he is also helping the world through him at that very time. When a mast thus surrenders his mind for the work of the Master, he is, in fact, getting closer to the Master as Truth. He is being perfected far more rapidly than would have been the case if he had avoided such surrender.

So the Master's activity with masts is two-fold, helping mankind through the masts, and—in reward for his co-operation as it were—helping the mast himself.

Exactly how Baba helped mankind by means of the masts is, of course, his own secret. But it has been suggested that the masts serve as what might be called, by a rather strained metaphor, 'spiritual dynamos'. We are familiar with the idea of contemplative orders in the Christian religion, monks and nuns who do not involve themselves in charitable work, believing they do more for their fellowmen and women through prayer than by attempts to relieve distress directly. Masts, particularly those who have attained high levels of development, have freed themselves from the commonplace desires which clutter up the mind of normal man, and in so doing turned themselves into spiritual channels, through which divine power and love can flow into the world. It is not as a rule so flowing because, in becoming 'God-intoxicated' the mast has not only lost consciousness of himself but of the needs of humanity at large. If this is a true picture, Baba's work with a mast can be compared to the clearing of an irrigation channel.

"I love them, and they love me. I help them, and they help me," was Baba's own simple statement. But years later, at the great sahavas or gathering in India in 1955, he expanded this:

> My love for the masts is similar in many ways to that shown by a mother who continues to look lovingly after her children regardless of their behaviour. To make her child clean a mother does not even mind soiling her hands with the child's excrement. I am the mother of the masts. They are also like parts of my body. Some are like my right and some are like my left limbs and fingers. Some are nose, ears and eyes for me. I am helpful to them and they are helpful to me. The masts alone know how they love me and I alone know how I love

them. I work for the masts, and knowingly or unknowingly they work for me.*

It has been suggested—though not by Dr Donkin—that through these 'spiritual dynamos', Baba exerted his influence on events in the external world. "The Mad Ashram was one of the activities in Baba's spiritual programme to restore normality to a war-crazy world,"† and C. B. Purdom, in his book *The God-Man*, seeks to establish a correlation between world events and specific phases of the mast work. Whether such connection can be established or not, it would certainly seem that Baba's periods of intensest work among the masts coincided with the tensest crises of the war and the years of 'near-war' which followed. "Between 11 and 20 March [1940]," Purdom records, "all at Meherabad had been made to fast because, said Baba, a matter of great importance in the war was about to take place. Indeed, it was so, for preparations were in hand for the great campaigns of Germany in Europe, when the Low Countries were over-run, France was laid low, and the British evacuated from Dunkirk."

Finally, there appears also to have existed a special relationship, inexplicable by our notions of cause and effect, between individual masts and certain countries. An example of this was the great mast Chatti Baba and his connection with France. Though literate, Chatti Baba never to anyone's knowledge saw a newspaper or had any means of information about current events. Yet, in the early part of 1940 at the Meherabad ashram, he repeatedly told his attendant that the peoples of Europe were undergoing great suffering, but would survive to enjoy happy days again. One day, pouring earth over his head, he said that there would be much anguish and privation, and many would perish of starvation, but that Baba would finally assuage the suffering of the world. However, on the night of 9th June, 1940,‡ Chatti Baba became suddenly violent and abusive. Rushing from his room in a frenzy, he went to Baba's room, saying that he had come for shelter since his own home was utterly destroyed. Baba at once gave orders that they were to be left alone together, and Chatti Baba could be heard arguing and expostulating with him for some hours. At last he became quiet,

* *Listen, Humanity*, by Meher Baba. Narrated and edited by D. E. Stevens, p. 260.
† *Meher Baba on War*: Meher Era Publication, Poona, 1972.
‡ It may be recalled that the collapse of the French Army began about 5th June 1940, and the Germans entered Paris eight days later.

spent the rest of the night alone with Baba, and in the morning returned to his own room, which, so far from being 'utterly destroyed' was just as neat and orderly as it had always been.

Baba then explained to the mandali that it was Chatti Baba's spiritual connection with France, and the disaster which was at that moment overwhelming that country, which filled him with despair.

Chapter 10

'HELPLESS AND HOPELESS'

During 1948 it became plain to those about Baba that a new phase of his work was starting. In June–July he called upon all followers throughout the world for special abstinence "because spiritually this is a period of crisis". On New Year's Day 1949, he sent them all a warning that a great personal disaster was coming upon himself; that the mandali would be faced with severe trials which only a few might be able to endure; he called upon "all men and women who believe in me" to observe a full month's silence during the coming July, and he repeated his ban on political activities. Meantime Baba continued his mast tours as strenuously as ever until June when he went into seclusion. He is described at this time as having "the bearing of one who had succeeded in a great campaign. There was great peace about him, his gaze penetrating and glowing, his mien alert, his hair short and manageable, with a pigtail."

Baba had entered upon many seclusions and would enter upon many more, but this of June–July 1949, because of the work to be accomplished, was regarded by him as 'The Great Seclusion'. It took place at Meherazad, not in any building but inside the body of that renowned blue motor-bus in which so many mast tours had been conducted. Worn out with years of journeying, overloaded, over every kind of road, it had been removed from its wheels, mounted on oil drums and built in with brick and lime. The seclusion was for forty days. At times Baba fasted completely, at others took only liquids or food once a day. A continual watch was maintained outside the bus with total silence, and it was noticed that whereas normally Baba would sleep for an hour or an hour and a half each night, he appeared now never to sleep for more than a few minutes. Of the first spell of seclusion he said later: "No one except God and myself knows what I went through during those nine days." Yet when the full forty days were up he emerged at the hour fixed "a picture of health and radiance".

A New Life was to begin, he told his followers. To all who accepted Baba as the Avatar its keynote must have sounded strange: "I shall be absolutely helpless in the true and literal sense of the word on account of some personal disaster to me." Before that happened Baba ceased to apply himself to any material affairs: "Everything I possess including ashram buildings, fields and houses, both here and elsewhere, and all furniture, cars, power-plants, cattle, chattels and in fact everything that belongs to me, is to be disposed of. Nothing is to remain as my property and in my name except the Meherabad Hill premises on which the tomb for my bodily remains has already been built...." A deadline of the 15th October was fixed by which all arrangements had to be completed. "I want to be absolutely free from everything and everybody. There will be no compromise now about anything. I am becoming *ghutt* [hardened], *naffat* [callous], and penniless. Remember the proverb *Nanga-se-Khuda bhi darta hai* [even God is afraid of the naked]."*

Three alternatives were offered to the mandali. To go with Baba, face all the difficulties of their choice and literally beg their bread with him from day to day; to earn their own living in the world and spare what they could for the support of dependent families, while continuing to obey all Baba's orders; or to leave and go their own way. Everyone had been warned to be absolutely honest in giving his opinion. "Don't be vague. Say exactly what you think and how you feel. You should not say 'Baba, your will'." A similar choice was set before the women mandali, with one difference, that they might if they wished leave all decision to Baba. But even in abdicating decision they must take responsibility for such abdication, since every man or woman was obliged to accept responsibility for his or her course of action on oath before God.

Sarosh, that same Sarosh who as a young man had so often found his bedding-roll thrown out by his Master, was now a prosperous business man besides being one of the mandali. He at once offered to maintain indefinitely all men and women who remained with Baba. Baba smiled his approval of the offer, but told Sarosh he had 'missed the whole point' of his instructions.

---

* Baba once explained: "To be empty means to be rid of all desires, and concerns the heart. To be naked concerns the mind, and means not to care for the opinions, criticism, or censure of others in one's pursuit" (of the True Goal).

Proceeds from the sale of all properties were to be set aside to support those *not* going with Baba, but for those who chose to remain with him no provision whatever must be made. "I and those who are going with me are going to suffer. We are going to start without any protection. We shall have to go a-begging."

At a solemn ceremony on the 18th August, Baba offered up a prayer, read out from his dictation on the alphabet board: "May God help Baba to definitely make this step, which he is taking to give up everything and to go away, irrevocable, so that from the 16th October when he enters the new life, there will be no turning back." This was the first prayer from Baba to God for help which the mandali had heard for twenty-eight years, and they were so astonished that no one could even say 'Amen'. Eruch, in a recent interview, suggested as reason for this 'human' prayer: "Baba during the New Life did not want his companions to accept him as the God-man. To them he was one of the companions. When he came down from the highest level to the level of a Perfect Person he invoked the blessing of God as any ordinary man would."*

At a further ceremony on the 31st August, in the presence of thirty-two persons—the only ones he had chosen out of 1,200 who in past times had sworn to follow his instructions—Baba himself took a solemn oath to lead the New Life till the end. Once again he warned those present that their decision would be binding for all time, and that anyone not prepared for a life of absolute obedience and sacrifice would do better to remain behind. All present then withdrew to make up their minds, and three hours later, when all decisions had been handed in, it appeared that sixteen men and four women were resolved to accompany Baba into the New Life.

Meantime Baba's instructions for the disposing of all property were being literally carried out. "Everything in Meherabad which was not personally used by Baba had to be sold. . . . Brass pots, pans, kettles, tea-sets, cutlery, glassware, carpets, presents given by the Western disciples or by Eastern devotees, were brought out and packed to be sent to Bombay by truck. Some might mumble, 'You'll not be able to get another kettle like this one, or knives like this,' to be hushed by others with 'It doesn't matter, we never used them anyway.' Mehera and some of the others gave costly silk sarees and any jewellery they had.

---

* Eruch Jessawala, in an interview with Naosherwan Anzar, *The Glow*. February 1973.

Furniture, beds, cupboards, everything went into the jackpot. From Meherazad also articles were sent—the brand-new refrigerator that Elizabeth [Patterson] had ordered from America and her two De Soto cars which she had given to Baba and a small car which Nariman had presented."*

Excitement mounted as the day fixed drew near, and at last in the earliest hours of the morning of the 16th October under the driving rain of the monsoon, the party started off. Partly on foot and partly by bus and rail they made their way across India, arriving early on the morning of the 15th November at the holy city of Benares, where an old house with a large garden had been taken for the party. Divested of all belongings, they had now to support themselves by begging, and trust, like the disciples sent out by Jesus, that their needs would be provided for. Like those disciples also, they were sent out in pairs and under stringent orders. They were to accept nothing except food, and any money must be refused. On receiving a gift they must come away immediately; if rejected they must go to the next house. When both had received 'Bhiksha' (alms), they should return directly to headquarters. They were not allowed to beg from acquaintances or from shops. Moreover, when they moved on from place to place, no food must be preserved for the next day, "Every day will be a new day for us in this New Life". On a number of days Baba himself shared in the ordeal of begging, barefoot and bareheaded, dressed in white, carrying a brass bowl and a cotton bag, with an ochre satchel over his left arm.

Benares is a city of beggars. Since the mandali were clearly not ordinary paupers, yet were forbidden to mention Baba's name or offer any explanation, they had a far from easy time. One well-dressed man rounded on two of the disciples, telling them they should be ashamed to be seen begging and ought to go and find themselves a job. Two others, stout to begin with and looking stouter because they were wearing all the clothes they had, were ridiculed: "You look like wrestlers—go and work for your living!" On the other hand a poor village woman, having said she had no food in the house and nothing to cook with, urged the disciples to wait, borrowed what she could from a neighbour and prepared vegetables and bread which Baba himself shared out among them all.

On the 1st December the party moved to Sarnath, a few miles north, where they lived in two small bungalows. All spare

---
* *The Glow*, February 1973.

'HELPLESS AND HOPELESS'

clothing and last vestiges of the 'old life' had now been discarded, but something else had been acquired, a small horde of animals— a white horse, a camel and camel-cart, a caravan pulled by oxen for the women, a bullock cart, two donkeys, two cows, and a calf which, when tired, had to be carried on someone's shoulders. All inevitably had to be fed, and before leaving Sarnath all the party except three were asked to surrender their wrist-watches to raise money, which they immediately did.

One of the most difficult tasks for the party was the remaining cheerful under all conditions insisted on by Baba. "I am expecting of you in this New Life something which is superhuman in some aspects," he told them. "I am in the soup too along with you. To keep cheerful under all circumstances is superhuman. Let us therefore do our best to help each other. I help you, you help me, in order to uphold each other's oath. The most important point that would carry you through safely with me, is to have no moods.... Even if moods sometimes come and anger is stirred, never express them in any manner, covert or overt. It is all the play of the mind, and the mind, with a little conscientious effort, can be made to adapt itself."

Mani, Baba's sister, who was one of the four women companions, has left a vivid picture "...of those days when the discipline and privations were extreme, as was the feeling of freedom and inner satisfaction." She tells of "seemingly non-stop walking by day, and of nights spent in a disused barn or schoolhouse or stable, or again (as so often) under the trees in a mango orchard with far from sufficient covering to ward off the bitter cold and heavy dew.... Baba would usually walk ahead with Eruch, we women a little distance behind, with the rest of the procession following last. Baba never appeared to be walking fast, just to be walking on air with that strong, graceful stride, while our pace was too obviously hurried. And as the miles would vanish, miles of often beautiful countryside, we lesser companions would not unnaturally find our thoughts dwelling more on food than nature's beauty...."

Eruch, in the interview previously quoted, gives the picture as the men saw it: "...we had absolutely no shelter over our heads, our food rations were inadequate, we walked in the rain, under the sun and were exposed to the elements. Moreover, we had a moral responsibility of looking after the women, and then again the fear that Baba would send us back if we showed any emotion or broke his orders. It will indeed be incomprehensible to those who have not been through this New Life, to visualise the tremendous suffering each one had to undergo, but this suffering was largely nullified by Baba's benign presence.... During the New Life we addressed Baba as our Elder Brother and Baba's identity was never revealed to anyone. He played the role of the elder brother to the hilt. He was our guide, our friend and above all our companion. During this companionship we loved each other, helped each other, despite the fact that each one of us had a different temperament. Baba brought us together into a cohesive whole; free of selfishness."

An intense devotion was aroused in the little band by their sense of Baba's presence continually among them, and his loving comradeship. "The elder companions—Gustadji, Patel and Anna 104, never once took a lift but walked all the way. Anna was known as 104 because once when he was ill at his home he kept telling everyone that his temperature was 104 and Baba gave him this nickname ... all day he would walk with the others and at night would sit outside Baba's tent to keep watch. He rested a while in the evening, but that hardly meant any rest. He said sitting and keeping watch and repeating Baba's name to himself was rest enough."*

This intensely exacting New Life was continued throughout 1950. Sometimes the begging regulations were relaxed or suspended for a short period and a degree of modest comfort permitted; sometimes they were intensified. Some of the companions left Baba for a while to go back to their homes or take up various employments. Enormous distances were covered—3,500 miles by train and on foot between 21st October and 6th December, 1950—and many masts and holy persons contacted. These contacts, Baba explained, were different from those made during the 'old life' since there was now no special work to be done with them. He contacted the masts to take their darshan,† which had significance for him, but what this significance was he did not explain, except to say that it had "nothing to do with spirituality". On occasions collections were made among the followers in India and overseas and considerable sums raised. In general these were used for distribution to the poor, to sufferers from famine and to victims of the disastrous floods. But once, when searching for poor people, Baba learned

---

* *The Glow*, February 1973.
† Literally: to have a sight or vision of someone devotionally: to place one's head on the feet of the revered one

of a man who had inherited several million rupees, wasted it all, and was now living with his wife in a hovel, a sick man. Baba sought him out, washed his feet, and gave him 300 rupees (£20–25). The man was so overcome that he collapsed, and Baba sat with him till he recovered consciousness.

If we should attempt an explanation of the inexplicable, we might say that the New Life was a living demonstration of the truth that all belongings constitute a tie, a tie to the superficial world and a barrier between us and reality. To 'find treasure in Heaven' we must first 'sell all that thou hast and give to the poor'. The corollary of which is that God always provides for those who make themselves utterly dependent upon him. It may be remembered that these years were ones in which, following the war in Europe and Asia and the consequences of partition and famine in India, millions of people had been uprooted from their homes, rendered 'helpless and hopeless' and forced to depend for their living upon charity. Over much of Asia this took the form of literally begging each day's bread; in Europe it took that of refugee camps dependent on overseas help, particularly on help from America under the Marshall Plan, and from the United Nations under the temporary organisation known as U.N.R.R.A.* In the mysterious way in which he operated, Baba was taking upon his own shoulders and those of the mandali the condition of the lost and unhappy peoples of the world. At the start of the New Life, Baba publicly put aside his condition as God to become a man among men, the 'Son of Man', the companion of his companions. He refused to allow anyone to bow down to him or pay marks of respect. He himself bowed down to the humblest, washed their feet and gave them alms from what he had, as testimony to the brotherhood of all men, and in humility before the Divine Spirit which is in every creature, however degraded and unaware of its presence we may be.

But it is not only material possessions which constitute a tie. We are tied by our desires and ambitions; even our hopes and spiritual aims can constitute fetters. In the New Life everything had to be given up—'No spiritual benefit' Baba insisted in each of the alternatives put before the mandali. Hopelessness and helplessness were to be literal and complete—even the hope of being alive tomorrow or of seeing Baba again must be abandoned. "I am going to see who is out to die for no reason by

* United Nations Relief and Rehabilitation Administration.

going with me." And he told the women mandali they were to give up hope wholeheartedly and sincerely of ever seeing and meeting him again. All trouble was from hoping: where there was no hope there could follow no disappointment. "Being with Baba and following him," says Eruch,* "meant renunciation which even involved renunciation. The very concept of renunciation had to be renounced... our sole object was to follow Baba to where he took us and to obey his every command."

In February 1951, his journeyings seemingly over for the present, Baba once more went into seclusion accompanied by fasting. In the middle of the year he called his disciples and devotees together, including those from the old life, and declared that a further step had been decided on. This would not be a step back from 'helplessness and hopelessness', but a step beyond, into complete mental annihilation, and Baba would, he said "in the natural course of events be facing physical annihilation as well, without my actually seeking it.... Anyone who wants to go through this dying process with me can join me; but I want everyone of you to understand fully the magnitude of the mental preparation needed to stand by such a decision.... If you choose to accompany me from mere emotional impulse, it will prove disastrous.... I shall have absolutely no responsibility and might have no concern whatever for anyone accompanying."

Despite these stern warnings, twenty-one men volunteered to go with Baba into the mental annihilation which he called *manonash*, and from them he chose eight for consideration before finally deciding upon five. All Baba's followers throughout the world were asked to participate in this further undertaking, first by a day of total silence on the 10th July, the anniversary of Baba's starting his own silence, and later from the end of December to mid-February 1952, by repeating the name of God as used by their own religion with whole-hearted devotion for half an hour each day.

On the last day of the year 1951, Baba dictated a statement which included the following:

To try to understand with the mind that which the mind can never understand, is futile; and to try to express by sounds of language and in forms of words the transcendent state of the soul, is even more futile. All that can be said, and has been

* *The Glow*, February 1973.

said, and will be said, by those who live and experience that state, is that when the false self is lost, the Real Self is found; that the birth of the Real can follow only the death of the false; and that dying to ourselves—the true death which ends all dying—is the only way to perpetual life. This means that when the mind with its desires, cravings and longings, is completely consumed by the fire of Divine Love, then the infinite, indestructible, indivisible, eternal Self is manifested. This is manonash, the annihilation of the false, limited, miserable, ignorant, destructible 'I', to be replaced by the real 'I', the eternal possessor of Infinite Knowledge, Love, Power, Peace, Bliss and Glory.... We are all in this shoreless ocean of Infinite Knowledge, and yet are ignorant of it until the mind—which is the source of ignorance—vanishes for ever; for ignorance ceases to exist when the mind ceases to exist.

To most of us this will seem a shattering statement. It is not ignorance but knowledge which, in our opinion, "ceases to exist when the mind ceases to exist". Mind, to us, is the source of all progress and development. We honour a man of great intellect, and there can be few actions more praiseworthy, we believe, than for a man or woman to develop his or her own mind by study, or that of their children through education. And indeed Baba himself insisted many times on the importance of mental effort and application. How then can it possibly be said that the mind is the source of ignorance and has to be annihilated?

The mind is the enemy of ultimate reality because through the mental processes our whole picture of life and our own place in it has been constructed on a false premise, that of each man's total separation from his neighbour. For every man, woman and child—through the operation of mind and the impressions it gathers in—life becomes 'myself as distinct from everybody and everything', and can all too easily become 'myself against everybody and everything'. The mind has separated the human race into classes, castes, tribes, nations, through all those multiple prejudices, customs, laws which we assume to be innate, but which have actually to be taught to children or newcomers. It is thus the mind which is responsible for most of the ills that destroy man's happiness and peace. The mind is the source of hatred, crime, competition based on greed, racial and national antagonisms, with the crushing burden for group protection of an ever-increasing load of armaments. Mind is the cause of war itself.

Conditioned to see life as duality and separation—just as a bird's eyes being set on each side of its head present it always with two different, unfocused views—the mind can admit no viewpoint but its own. It inevitably sets itself up as the sole judge of reality. Nothing is true which cannot be proved by its own system of tests. Nothing it cannot weigh or measure, demonstrate or detect, is allowed to have 'real' existence. And it is this attempt to claim absolute authority which makes mind 'the source of ignorance', since from the point of view of spirit those factors which can be weighed and measured are precisely those which have least importance. Moreover the basic truth of spirit, asserted by every great religion, is one which the dualistic mind by its very nature cannot accept. This is that unity of all life on which Baba continually insisted. So far from being completely separate individuals, we are all eternally one and indivisible; and every form of life down to the rocks and stones, and the gases from which solid matter originally took shape, is a form of spirit linked indissolubly with every other form.

"Reality," said Baba, "is beyond human understanding, for it is beyond reason. Understanding cannot help because God is beyond understanding. The moment you try to understand God you 'misunderstand' him; you miss him when you try to understand him. Reason must go before knowledge dawns.... Only manonash (annihilation of mind) takes one to reality. There is a way to annihilate the mind. The way is love. Just consider ordinary human love: when a man or woman is deeply in love with his or her partner, nothing comes between them. They get totally lost in love for one another. There is neither admiration nor fault-finding. There is total absence even of exchange of thought: love prevails without thoughts. Mind becomes defunct for the time being: for in such intense human love mind does not come into play.... If ordinary human love can go so far, what should be said of the height of love divine?"

Manonash, the elimination of mind in love, was the culmination of the New Life. And the New Life, in which all are companions, loving and serving one another, and dependent for each day's food and shelter upon God and the charity of fellowmen, has provided, perhaps, a glimpse into that New Age which Baba foretold will succeed the present one. This is an age in which intuition has superseded reason; love has conquered fear and greed; sharing has replaced competition and self-seeking; and all men—whether as individuals or nations—depend confidently on one another's generosity and love.

And the animals that accompanied Baba and the mandali into the New Life—what were they doing? That camel, the bullocks and cows, the calf that was always having to be carried, the white horse? They stood perhaps for the animal creation which must, since the universe is linked by spirit, share in and benefit from that raising of the spiritual climate brought about by the New Life. As indeed must also, in one way or another, the whole of our misused, exploited, eroded and polluted planet.

Chapter 11

THE 'GREAT PERSONAL DISASTER'

THE AVATAR IS both God and man. The kiss given to Baba as a boy by Hazrat Babajan had made him aware of his own Divinity, at an age when, as he said, "... I did not know anything. I had nothing to do with spirituality.... I preferred games." From the time of his recovery, after the long disturbance which followed his recognition of the task imposed on him, Baba had lived in the divine aspect of himself with unquestioned and unquestioning assurance and authority. Then during the period of the New Life, Baba had consciously and deliberately assumed humanity, and humanity at its most 'helpless and hopeless'. He had divested himself of all possessions. He had allowed, almost urged, those about him to leave him if they wished to; only those prepared to face every kind of hardship, and even death, were permitted to remain, and the number of these was finally whittled down to no more than four or five. Towards his companions he had put aside his own unique position. "I shall live amongst you," he said, "as one of you like a brother;" and when in the course of their travels some visitors who knew Baba came and asked for darshan, he turned away, saying, "I am pleased to have your darshan." Again and again he emphasised that the New Life was no kind of test: "I want you all to understand once and for all that I am completely serious about this New Life.... There is absolutely no question of any tests or trials. What is there left for tests or trials after all the years you have been with me?"

From that day in August 1949, when he had so astonished the mandali by his prayer to God for help, Baba repeated such prayers in public, using completely human terms. "I ask the most merciful God to forgive me and my companions for any shortcomings and any conscious and unconscious mistakes done singly or wholly or towards each other ... as also for any lustful, greedy or old life thoughts and desires....", ending with the words, "I forgive you my companions, and ask you all to forgive me and

I ask God to forgive us all, not merely by way of ceremony but as a whole-hearted pardon." To the mandali Baba stressed that neither they nor he could expect any kind of spiritual benefit from following the arduous course they had undertaken. In the routine of every day he worked exactly like the others, not only taking part in the begging which brought home their helplessness to all of them, but sweeping, carrying loads, washing utensils and helping in the kitchen.

In every way Baba accepted, and compelled those about him to accept, that he shared their common humanity and ours. The words of the song which he asked one of his companions, Dr Ghani, to repeat the evening before they began their begging ran:

> Old Life has passed in different ways;
> Today also has passed somehow;
> Tomorrow be damned! Who cares?

At the end of the four-month period of *manonash* which was the culmination of the New Life, Baba dictated a statement summing up what had been achieved; divinity and humanity were now entirely merged.

For these last four months, according to ordinary human standards, and by ways and means known to me, I have tried my utmost for the achievement of *manonash*, and I can say in all truth that I feel satisfied with the work done. This satisfaction is due to the feeling I have of having regained my old-life Meher Baba state. I have regained the Knowledge, Strength and Greatness that I had in the Old Life, and retained the ignorance, weakness and humility of the New Life. This union of the old and new life states has given birth to Life that is eternally old and new.

Life for me now means:

1 Free and obligationless life.
2 Life of a Master in giving orders; and of a Servant in all humility.
3 The feeling of absolute conviction that we are all eternally One, Indivisible and Infinite in essence; and with it a feeling of separateness from the real Omnipresent Self, through ignorance.

4 Life of God in essence, and of man in action.
5 Life of Strength born of inherent Knowledge of Oneness; and of weakness born of binding desires. . . .

Between the last day of 1951, when the above statement was dictated, and 16th February, 1952, Baba was in seclusion. Following that seclusion there began another phase of Baba's life and work; this was divided into three periods, in each of which freedom was stressed, and for each of which fixed dates were given. These dates were to prove deeply significant, particularly in view of the warnings he had recently expressed of some great danger he was facing.

Back on New Year's Day, 1949, before he embarked on this 'Great Seclusion', Baba had sent out from Meherazad a circular to all devotees and followers giving warning of 'a great personal disaster' to himself. In August of the same year, when preparations for the New Life were in hand, Baba had told the mandali that at some time after the 1st October, "I shall be absolutely helpless in the true and literal sense of the word on account of some personal disaster to me." And again on 28th June, 1951, shortly before the start of the four-month manonash period, Baba had caused a statement to be read out in the presence of many disciples and devotees. In this he spoke of his coming mental annihilation, and added that he would ". . . be facing physical annihilation as well, without my actually seeking it."

The three new periods now announced were the 'Complicated Free Life'; the 'Full Free Life'; and the 'Fiery Free Life'. The first of these would last from the 21st March to the 10th July—that is, from the vernal equinox when days and nights are of equal length throughout the world, to the anniversary of that day on which he had first entered on his silence. But for Baba, with his Persian background, the 21st March had a further significance, being the start of the Irani New Year, Persia's oldest festival, which dates back several thousand years and is observed in every home with great rejoicing.

During this first period, Baba said, "bindings are to dominate freedom". What did this mean? 'Bindings' carries a special significance for Baba followers. Bindings are the *Sanskaras*, attach-

THE 'GREAT PERSONAL DISASTER' 99

ments resulting from all the attractions and repulsions we experience in an earthly life. All our ideas, ambitions, hopes, fears, relationships together constitute a body of desires which manifests itself over succeeding lives as our 'predisposition', exercising an invisible influence over us from birth to death. The influence of sanskaras, Baba says, persists through many lives until they are weakened by time* and altered by change of heart, or until, if we should be so fortunate, they are unwound and dispelled by the help of a Perfect Master.

Did Baba's words then mean that between March and July destinies from the past would be working themselves out in a manner that would 'dominate' freedom in the present? And, since Baba as a Perfect Master had long since liberated himself from his own sanskaras, could this imply that during these months he would be voluntarily identifying himself with his human aspect and undergoing suffering in the body, in order to ease the burden on humanity of its bindings from the past?

From the 11th July to the 14th November, 'freedom would dominate bindings' in what Baba called the 'Full Free Life, a period perhaps of identification with the divine aspect of himself. Then on the 15th November would begin the 'Fiery Free Life' in which both aspects would be absorbed into one. For this Baba gave the following explanation:

> The consuming of freedom and bindings (which is characteristic of the Fiery Free Life) means that there is a complete blending of the God-state and the man-state, so that one does not live through opposition to the other, and there can be no question of the one encroaching upon the other.
>
> Spiritual freedom is essentially a positive state of conscious enjoyment of divinity. It does not have to maintain itself through the overcoming of any bindings, for these are not bindings of the soul in its essence, but temporary bindings of the body and the mind, which can in no way curtail the Bliss, Power or Understanding of conscious Divinity.... After the annihilation of the limited mind, the infinite consciousness of the soul, with all its Knowledge, Power and Bliss, remains unaffected by any weaknesses or diseases to which the body may yield as a result of natural laws....

* "If the fool would persist in his folly he would become wise." William Blake (1757–1827).

Side by side with other activities of the Fiery Free Life, there will be one constant feature of that life, wherever it takes me. I shall bow down to the saints whom I adore, the masts whom I worship, and the poor, to whom I am wholeheartedly devoted. Nothing makes me more happy than to bow down to God in all these forms."

These last sentences seemed to indicate that the Fiery Free Life would involve travel and many contacts, and it was significant that Baba had already sent Eruch and Pendu to visit places in India and Pakistan to make preparations.

The 21st March, 1952, was the date fixed for the start of that Complicated Free Life in which 'bindings were to dominate freedom', and in April Baba set out for the United States. "My work in the West will be done by women,"* he had declared, and in the same way that he sent two men throughout India to prepare for his Fiery Free Life, he had long since sent two women with a special charge to America. These were Elizabeth Patterson, a successful American businesswoman, and Princess Norina Matchabelli, wife of a Georgian diplomat, famous for having played the Madonna in Max Reinhardt's production of *The Miracle*. For the past few years, on Baba's instructions, they had been establishing a Meher Baba Centre at a place called Myrtle Beach, 500 acres in a beautiful setting on the coast of South Carolina. This was now complete and Baba, who arrived in New York with five members of the mandali and four women disciples on the 20th April, came on here with his party after only one night's rest. With them also were two women disciples from the West, Kitty Davy and Rano Gayley, and Delia de Leon who had joined them from England.

After a stay of one month in the new Centre, Baba sent some of the mandali on ahead to Myrtle Mount, a small estate over on the West Coast in California where the party would remain for a while. He himself and the others were to follow in two cars. Before setting out, Baba went up to Elizabeth who was sitting in the driver's seat and asked if she had her insurance policy with her. Hearing that it was at her house, he told her to stop there and pick it up. With them in the car were three of the women mandali who had chosen to follow Baba into the New Life (in which he would see, he had said, "who is out to die for no reason by going with me"), Mehera, Baba's sister

* *The Awakener*, vol. XIV, No. 2. "Memories of '52", by Filis Frederick.

Mani, and his niece Meheru. The fourth, Dr Gohar, was in a station-wagon driven by Sarosh, together with Kitty Davy, Delia de Leon and Rano Gayley. Three nights were spent at different stops on the long journey westward, and on the morning of the 24th May, Kitty Davy records: "We were up early as usual. About 5 a.m. the group stood waiting in front of the motel for Baba's signal to step into the cars. This morning Baba delayed starting however. He came out of his room and stood quite still for some minutes on the doorstep, withdrawn, sad and unusually still. No last minute questions, no haste to be off. Elizabeth sat at the wheel awaiting his signal. Ten minutes elapsed before Baba walked to his car, followed by the women. The rest of us got into Sarosh's car as before. After a short distance, Baba's car stopped suddenly and Baba got out and paced up and down on the right side of the road. We too got out and stood by our car. This happened twice..."

Elizabeth Patterson now continues the account: "It had rained the night before and Route No. 64 was slippery, oilslick. The shoulder of the road was not wide and there were ditches on either side. As we came up over the crest of a small hill a car came along driving on the left hand side of the road, going at a good clip. I started to slow up. The car continued without slowing up right at us on the left hand side of the road. At any instant I expected him to turn... at the last instant he saw us and put on the brakes, whirling around to take up the entire side of the road. The point of contact was my bumper which made him whirl all the more...."

Baba, sitting in front, was flung out by the impact. His arm and leg were fractured, his head cut. Mehera and Meheru were also thrown out and injured. Elizabeth at the wheel was badly hurt, arms and wrists fractured and some ribs broken. Only Mani, who had been sleeping, seemed unhurt. Baba, who had previously said that he must shed blood on American soil, was the only one who actually did so, a much worse disaster being averted by the fact that the ditch into which they were flung was unusually soft. Of the three men in the oncoming car not one was injured. "We learned later," Elizabeth writes, that the driver was a "Korean veteran, a double amputee, who was driving for the very first time that day, a car made especially for him; also he was used to driving on the left-hand side, in Japan.... My one feeling was 'Don't go into the ditch!' Just before it happened Baba stretched out his hand and pointed at the oncoming car."

Delia de Leon recalls: "Baba had warned in India that an accident would befall him, but none of us gave it serious thought, though he kept warning us that we must keep with his car and not get lost, or he would never forgive us...." During the morning the party in the following car stopped for a cold drink, and then put on speed in order to catch up. "We could see no sign of his car and were beginning to get worried. It was about 10.05 a.m. We heard an exclamation of alarm from Sarosh. We turned our heads to the right. At first we could not take in what had happened; we could not see clearly from the car. We saw people standing round Baba who seemed to be lying on the ground. The women were lying in various directions. Sarosh exclaimed, 'O God, there's been an accident'... We dashed to the spot—and I can remember so vividly the extraordinary expression on Baba's face—his eyes unseeing ... far away."

The first person to bring help was a man on his way into the little town of Prague, Oklahoma, seven miles away, where he was taking his wife to have a baby. He ordered out two ambulances which carried the injured to a small private hospital run by a Dr Burleson. Here they were excellently cared for, but it was two weeks before the party could leave, travelling by ambulance the 1,500 miles back to Myrtle Beach where they slowly recovered. In a letter dated 3rd June, 1952, Dr Burleson wrote to Baba: "From you and your party we have seen a demonstration of most of the teachings of Christ. Many Americans preach these things but we have never observed so close an application of them. The profound devotion to you which is demonstrated by all your party convinces us that you deserve all of it. Such devotion cannot be forced, it can only be obtained by love; and to have that demonstrated affection from so many wonderful people is almost unbelievable. We are not accustomed to dealing with people who appreciate our efforts as you do, and the manifestation of this appreciation leaves us very humble...."

On the 13th June, Baba dictated a message to his followers. "The personal disaster for some years* foretold by me has at last happened while crossing the American continent, causing me through facial injuries, a broken leg and arm, much mental and physical suffering. It was necessary that it should happen in America. God willed it so.

"It brings to fruition the first part of the circular which said that until the 10th July (in the Complicated Free Life),

* It was originally foretold in 1928.

THE 'GREAT PERSONAL DISASTER' 103

weakness would dominate strength and bindings would dominate freedom; but from the 10th July in my Full Free Life, strength would dominate weakness and freedom would dominate bindings; and then, from the 15th November, in my Fiery Free Life, both strength and weakness, freedom and bindings would be consumed in the fire of Divine Love."

When sufficiently recovered, Baba returned to New York where he attended a number of meetings and gave interviews. From there on the 31st July he flew to London, staying for six days at the Hotel Rubens near Victoria, and giving interviews in, of all surprising places, one of those private rooms at the Charing Cross Hotel whose normal use was for small company meetings or salesmen's conferences. It was here that many of his British followers, including the two writers of this book, saw Baba for the first time. He was still in pain with his leg encased in plaster, but he was cheerful and full of energy, seeing everyone who wished to see him. A number of entertainments had been arranged before Baba's injury was known, and he insisted on going through with the programme in case his companions might be disappointed. Among the shows to which he was taken were the circus, a 'spectacular' on ice, and the musical *South Pacific*. Baba's own interest, one may imagine, being mainly in the large rapt audiences and the opportunity to make contact while their outward attention was absorbed. On the 6th August, the party left for Switzerland, from where they flew back two weeks later to Bombay.

In November began the Fiery Free Life and a spell of intense public activity. During the New Life period Baba had appeared to give his attention first to the mandali and the companions who travelled with him. It was this, they all agreed, which not only made their hardships bearable but the whole experience richly rewarding, so that they spoke and wrote of it afterwards like soldiers recalling an arduous but triumphant campaign. Now it was the turn of the masses, who for some years had not been allowed to visit freely, and to whom Baba had seldom given any mass darshan. Now for a number of weeks he travelled up and down India, stopping in towns and visiting villages where no car had been before. Wherever Baba arrived, he first sought out any masts or saints and contacted them before his presence could be generally known. Later, seated on a dais, he would receive the men, women and children of the place and the hundreds, sometimes thousands, who came pouring in from the surrounding countryside on foot, horseback, in carts drawn by bullocks and camels. Some of the people had been waiting for years simply to set eyes on Baba. One man came from a distance of twenty-seven miles rolling on the ground, not taking any food till he reached Baba.

After a whole day spent amongst the crowds, Baba would spend the next one going round individual homes, seeking out those who had not been able to attend the general gathering. As always he paid particular attention to the poor, bowing down to them, washing their feet and giving them money. This was not a demonstration for effect; nor was it what we in the West call 'charity'. The poor, Baba said, share his burden for the spiritual upliftment of humanity. He bowed to them out of gratitude, out of worship to the God that is in them, and "I did it with all my heart."

In Delhi, where about 3,000 students from a Sikh college gathered to meet him with their principal, Baba gave the following message:

India has gained its national freedom. Let us now try to gain our spiritual freedom beside which every other kind of freedom is a binding.... The purpose of life is to realise God within ourselves. This can be done even whilst attending to our worldly duties. In the everyday walks of life and amidst intense activities, we should feel detached and dedicate our doings to our Beloved God. Enough has been said to make people food-minded. They must now be made God-minded.

I give my love and blessings to one and all for the understanding of the One Infinite God residing equally within us all, and beside whom everything else is false and illusory.

Chapter 12

THE AVATAR

DURING THE YEARS following his return after his injury, Baba held a number of gatherings, mainly in India but also in the United States, besides paying shorter visits to Europe and Australia. At these gatherings, known as 'sahavas', he made a series of statements plain enough for a child to understand, but with a power and authority unheard for two thousand years, covering the whole field of human life and of man's relationship with God. These were made partly through prepared discourses read out to his assembled followers, and partly in exchange of talk and answers to questions from his audience. In both, certain themes constantly recur.

Man's need to get rid of the false self (ego), and liberate the true self (spirit) which is in every one of us. It is the ego which keeps man in a state of conflict and separation, while spirit seeks always to unite. The way to achieve this liberation is through love. Love, in the word's true meaning, is not something which appears naturally in us like eyesight. It has to be diligently sought, in the first place through service to others: "Emotion is not bad, but love is quite different."

The need for honesty towards ourselves, others, and towards God—"God forgives everything except hypocrisy"—and for obedience among those claiming to be his followers. "Obedience is more than love. Love is a gift from the Beloved to the lover, whereas obedience is an offering from the lover to the Beloved."

Above all, he spoke of the role of the Avatar or God-Man, which is to awaken in man the knowledge of his own true nature. By arousing love and a passion for service in his heart, the Avatar helps man to draw closer and closer to the divine within him, and so over countless centuries to become God-realised—oneness with God being the sole purpose of life.

In September 1953, the 'Fiery Free Life' in which would come about "a complete blending of the God-state and the man-state" reached its climax. And at Dehra Dun, centre of country sacred to Siva, on the 7th September, reputed anniversary of the birth of Zoroaster, founder of the Zoroastrian or Parsi religion into which Baba had been born, he made an explicit statement of his own position as the latest, though not the last in the succession of Avataric appearances on earth:

> When God manifests on earth in the form of man and reveals his Divinity to mankind, he is recognised as the Avatar. . . .
> The Avatar is always one and the same, because God is always One and the Same, the Eternal, Indivisible, Infinite One. . . . This Eternally One and Same Avatar repeats his manifestation from time to time, in different cycles, adopting different human forms and different names, in different places . . . in order to raise humanity from the pit of ignorance and free it from the bondage of delusions.
> Of the most recognised and much worshipped manifestations of God as Avatar, that of Zoroaster is the earlier—having been before Rama, Krishna, Buddha, Jesus and Mohammed. Thousands of years ago he gave to the world the essence of Truth in the form of three fundamental precepts—Good Thoughts, Good Words and Good Deeds. These precepts were and are constantly unfolded to humanity in one form or another, directly or indirectly in every cycle, by the Avatar of the Age, as he leads humanity towards the Truth. . . . But to live up to these precepts honestly and literally is apparently as impossible as it is to practise a living death in the midst of life. . . .

Baba went on to declare that he was not one of the countless sadhus, saints, mahatmas, yogis of whom the world is full, and that if he is not to be included in their ranks, the question inevitably arises,

> What am I? The natural assumption would be that I am either just an ordinary human being, or I am the Highest of the High. . . .
> Now, if I am just an ordinary man, my capabilities and powers are limited—I am no better or different from an ordinary human being. If people take me as such they should not expect supernatural help from me in the form of miracles or spiritual guidance; and to approach me to fulfil their desires would also be absolutely futile.

On the other hand, if I am beyond the level of an ordinary human being, and much beyond the level of saints and yogis, then I must be the Highest of the High. . . .

If I am the Highest of the High my Will is Law, my wish governs the Law, and my Love sustains the Universe. Whatever your apparent calamities and transient sufferings, they are but the outcome of my Love for the ultimate good. Therefore, to approach me for deliverance from your predicaments, to expect me to satisfy your worldly desires, would be asking me to undo what I have already ordained. . . .

Know you all that if I am the Highest of the High, my role demands that I strip you of all possessions and wants, consume your desires and make you desireless rather than satisfy your desires. . . .

Mere intellectuals can never understand me through their intellect. If I am the Highest of the High, it becomes impossible for the mind to gauge me, nor is it possible for my ways to be fathomed by the human mind.

I am not to be attained by those who, loving me, stand reverently by in rapt admiration. I am not for those who ridicule me and point at me with contempt. To have a crowd of tens of millions flocking round me is not what I am for. I am for the few who, scattered amongst the crowd, silently and unostentatiously surrender their all—body, mind and possessions—to me. I am still more for those who, after surrendering their all, never give another thought to their surrender. . . .

From my point of view, far more blessed is the atheist who confidently discharges his worldly responsibilities, accepting them as his honourable duty, than the man who presumes he is a devout believer in God, yet shirks the responsibilities apportioned to him through Divine Law, and runs after sadhus, saints and yogis, seeking relief from the suffering which ultimately would have pronounced his eternal liberation.

To have one eye glued on the enchanting pleasures of the flesh and with the other expect to see a spark of Eternal Bliss is not only impossible but the height of hypocrisy. . . .

At Rajamundry to a gathering of his workers from Andhra State, which began at nine one evening and continued until three next morning, Baba urged uncompromising honesty towards his claims.

Do not propagate what you do not feel. What your heart says and what your conscience dictates about me, pour out without hesitation. But unmindful of whether you are ridiculed or accepting in pouring out your heart for me, or against me, to others.

If you take Baba as God, say so; do not hesitate.

If you think Baba is the Devil, say it. Do not be afraid.

I am everything that you take me to be, and I am also beyond everything.... Of myself I say again and again "I am the Ancient One—the Highest of the High."

These explicit and forceful statements had been made in India and to Indians. But now, in June 1954, Baba sent out invitations to selected people from the West as well as from India and Pakistan, to attend a 'meeting of meetings' in September. This was to be all-male, with no one present under sixteen years of age. From the East some thousand assembled, and from the West a handful of seventeen men. They were present at the last mass darshan where, to a gathering of some ten thousand people, Baba's message was broadcast.

Age after age, amidst the clamour of disruptions, wars, fear and chaos, rings the Avatar's call: 'Come all unto Me'.

Although, because of the veil of illusion, this call of the Ancient One may appear as a voice in the wilderness, its echo and re-echo nevertheless pervades through time and space, to rouse at first a few, and eventually millions, from their deep slumber of ignorance. And in the midst of illusion, as the Voice behind all voices, it awakens humanity to bear witness to the manifestation of God amidst mankind.

The time is come. I repeat the Call, and bid all to come unto me.... I tell you with all my Divine authority, that you and I are not 'We' but 'One'.... There is nothing but God. He is the only Reality, and we all are one in the indivisible Oneness of this absolute Reality....

Awaken from your ignorance, and try at least to understand that in the uncompromisingly Indivisible Oneness, not only is the Avatar God, but also the ant, and the sparrow, just as one and all of you are nothing but God. The only apparent difference is in the states of consciousness. The Avatar knows that that which is a sparrow is not a sparrow, whereas the sparrow does not realise this, and, being ignorant of its ignorance, remains a sparrow.

Live not in ignorance. Do not waste your precious life-span in differentiating and judging your fellowmen, but learn to long for the love of God. Even in the midst of your worldly activities, live only to find and realise your true Identity with your Beloved God.

Be pure and simple, and love all because all are one. Live a sincere life; be natural and be honest with yourself.

To those attending the sahavas Baba showed concern for every detail of their health and comfort, urging them too to be completely open and to speak their minds. "If the food does not agree with you, say so. If there is anything you don't like, say so. Don (Dr Donkin) is in charge of your health. If you have any difficulty of any kind, tell him. . . . After all, you have come a great distance to attend these meetings, and I want you to receive as much as you possibly can from them. When they are over, I want you to go home as quickly and directly as possible, so that you can carry with you, still fresh, what you have received."

The visitors from the West were with Baba for some three weeks, during which time he gave them an intimacy of personal contact: "I am your Master, but I am also your friend. I am one of you, and one with you." He talked to them about his early life, about the nature of the universe, about the differences between states of trance and true God-realisation. At times he revealed an almost child-like aspect of himself.

Sometimes I feel, why explain anything? Just come, sit down, you all here. Be quiet and be in company with Baba. Sometimes I feel like explaining things. I wonder which is better. What shall we do? Shall we go on explaining things, or shall we be quiet?

At times his humour showed through unexpectedly. When one of his devotees read out in Sanskrit a passage from the Bhagavad Gita in which Krishna speaks of the coming of the Avatar; "Age after age, from time immemorial, for the destruction of ignorance, for the preservation of Truth, I have taken human form", Baba remarked when he had finished: "You say this as if you were swimming in mid-ocean and attacked by sharks." He then added wryly: "I have created everything, and yet I don't know Sanskrit. I just nod my head as if I knew."*

As the final act in this 'meeting of meetings', at 3.0 p.m. on Thursday, 30th September, 1954, Eruch read out Meher Baba's Final Declaration:†

> I have not come to establish anything new—I have come to put life into the old.... When my universal religion of love is on the verge of fading into insignificance, I come to breathe life into it and to do away with the farce of dogmas that defile it in the name of religions and stifle it with ceremonies and rituals....
>
> Suffering in the world is at its height, in spite of all the striving to spread peace and prosperity to bring about lasting happiness.... To affirm religious faiths, to establish societies, or to hold conferences will never bring about the feeling of unity and oneness in the life of mankind.... I have come to sow the seed of love in your hearts so that, in spite of all superficial diversity which your life in illusion must experience and endure, the feeling of oneness, through love, is brought about amongst all the nations, creeds, sects and castes of the world.

And Baba went on to make one of his mysterious references to the end of his silence and the Word which he would speak.

> In order to bring this about, I am preparing to break my silence. When I break my silence it will not be to fill your ears with spiritual lectures. I shall speak only one Word, and this Word will penetrate the hearts of all men and make even the sinner feel that he is meant to be a saint, while the saint will know that God is in the sinner as much as he is in himself.
>
> When I speak that Word, I shall lay the foundation for that which is to take place during the next seven hundred years. When I come again after seven hundred years the evolution of consciousness will have reached such an apex that materialistic tendencies will be automatically transmuted into spiritual longing, and the feeling of equality in spiritual brotherhood will prevail. This means that opulence and poverty, literacy and illiteracy, jealousy and hatred, which are

---

* The languages Baba spoke were Persian, English, Hindi, Gujerati, Urdu and Marathi.
† This is given in full in C. B. Purdom's *The God-Man*, pp. 272–5.

in evidence today in their full measure, will then be dissolved through the feelings of the oneness of all men. Prosperity and happiness will then be at their zenith. . . .

The Declaration, which was read out in English, and then translated into Hindi, Marathi, Gujerati and Telegu, was received in complete silence. Following it, the whole company broke up and went to their own homes.

Chapter 13

A 'SO-CALLED TRAGEDY'

FOR THREE MONTHS, in the middle of 1955, Baba was in seclusion, but towards the end of that year he gave sahavas at Meherabad. These were attended by an American devotee, Don Stevens, who has written a full and illuminating account in his book *Listen, Humanity*.* At these sahavas, given largely for his Indian followers, Baba stressed the importance of living in the world and not retreating from it. Among those attending was one, Mouni Baba, who had been keeping silence for many years. Baba ordered him to speak, which he did, just as on other occasions he had ordered a holy man to eat or to take a drink. Later Baba told the company:

> The whole of creation is a play of thoughts: the outcome of the mind. It is your mind that binds you; it is also the mind that is the means of your freedom.... The best way to cleanse the heart and to prepare for the stilling of the mind is to lead a normal life in the world. Living in the midst of your day-to-day duties, responsibilities, likes and dislikes, becomes the very means for the purification of your heart.
>
> For the purification of your heart, leave your thoughts alone but maintain constant vigil over your actions. Let thoughts come and go without putting them into action.
>
> It is better to feel angry sometimes rather than merely to repress anger. Although your mind may be angry do not let your heart know it. Remain unaffected. If you never feel angry you will be like stone, in which form the mind is least developed.
>
> Let the thoughts of anger, lust and greed come and go freely without putting them into words and deeds. Then the related impressions in your mind begin to wear out and become less harmful.

* *Listen, Humanity*, by Meher Baba, narrated and edited by D. E. Stevens. Dodd Mead & Co., New York, 1957.

When you feel angry or have lustful thoughts, remember Baba at once. Let my name serve as a net around you.

Early in 1956 Baba went into retirement at Satara, and on the 15th February he said that he would be in complete retirement for one year, except for a visit to the West which he had promised for July. As the time for this approached, Baba sent out a message to his Western followers:

> ... a great so-called tragedy is facing me and my lovers. My long-expected humiliation is near at hand. This may happen tomorrow or any day of this year, or it may happen next year.
> The love, courage and faith of my lovers will be put to a severe test, not by me, but by Divine Law.

In mid-July 1956 Baba was in London, staying at the Hotel Rubens, near Victoria. There had been conflict in the British group and Baba devoted a morning to listening to the views of those involved. He obliged all to speak out openly, voicing their criticisms in front of one another. Finally he issued clear-cut instructions for future working, and personally arranged a transfer of funds to put the group back on its feet. Throughout his short stay Baba showed that attention to detail and insistence on efficiency with which his mandali were already familiar. He was at work by 5.0 a.m., and if he ordered a meeting for 9.0 a.m. he was in the room as the clock was striking.

For the evening reception, held in one of the hotel's largest rooms, a British devotee had arranged a spectacular setting. Against a background of purple hangings, on a settee placed in the centre of one wall, covered with glowing satin and velvet cushions and flanked with massive flower displays, Baba looked truly regal. Some two hundred followers came up one by one to be greeted. It was a moving scene, and for most of those present it formed their last visual memory of their Master, since he never came back again to Britain.

From London Baba flew to New York where he stayed a week, followed by another at Myrtle Beach, and then went on to Australia. By mid-August he was back in India, in seclusion at Satara. In the last days of November he told those about him that the month or so preceding the end of his seclusion on 15th February, 1957, would hold increased and concentrated suffering for himself, in which a number of his close ones would also share.

On Sunday, the 2nd December, Baba was returning to Satara from a day's visit to Poona. It was a dull, overcast day, with no traffic and scarcely any foot-passengers on the road. Eruch, skilled and careful, who had driven Baba many thousands of miles, was at the wheel with Baba beside him. In the back sat three of the mandali, Pendu, Vishnu and Dr Nilkanth, known as 'Nilu'. Suddenly, as they were running easily and at moderate speed, the car got out of control and crashed against a low stone culvert, overturning and flinging most of its occupants out. This happened at about 1.15 p.m. The road was good and there was nothing in sight, no other vehicle, no walkers, not even a stray goat or a squawking hen. There was neither puncture nor skidding, the speed was under 40 miles an hour and the car had previously been in good order. Eruch said later that the driving wheel "seemed to stop co-ordinating", the car swerved straight towards the culvert, and he remembered no more till he came to. The accident was as serious as it was inexplicable. Baba's face and head were badly hurt and his tongue torn, in addition he sustained damage to his right hip, which later proved to be a fracture of the upper end of the thigh. Eruch suffered four broken ribs, Pendu and Vishnu were somewhat less seriously hurt, but Nilu was unconscious and seemed seriously injured.

Vishnu, on coming to, found himself alone in the back of the car. He got out, went to the front and saw Baba in the front seat with blood on his clothes and face. After some moments he asked Baba if he was badly hurt. Baba nodded, pointing to his mouth and leg, but indicated to Vishnu to attend first to the three who had been flung out. Eruch meantime, with a tremendous effort, had managed to stand up and speak to Baba, supporting himself against the car. Three minutes after the crash a man going to Poona came along, lifted Baba and Vishnu into his own car, and drove them back down the road to Satara. Not long after a truck arrived and carried the three others to the mandali's quarters. Eruch and Pendu were at once taken to hospital, but Nilu died in the truck without regaining consciousness.

Some days previous to the accident Baba had smilingly told the mandali, "We may all die in a few days." Turning to Nilu he added, "Don't worry about anything. Keep thinking of me constantly. I am the only One that exists, the only One that matters." During his period in hospital after the accident, Baba said of Nilu's death, "It is as he would have wanted it. He is blessed to be with me."

This period, winter 1956, was that of the Hungarian rising and its harsh suppression by the Russians, and the morning after the crash, Baba made one of his rare comments on public affairs, for though in normal circumstances he followed the day-to-day progress of events closely, he almost never spoke of them except in general terms. But now he said with gestures to those about him: "The Hungarians suffered much in their recent struggle. Many were lying wounded and helpless on the roads, away from their loved ones and from care or relief from pain. At least I am lying on a bed, with the care of good doctors and the love of all my lovers, present and absent."

The injuries to Baba's face and mouth required stitching but did not take long to heal. What proved far more difficult to treat was the damage to his hip. After a week in Satara, when complications had set in and the pain was exceedingly severe, Baba accepted the doctor's pleas that he should be conveyed to Poona where better facilities existed. Here the plaster cast into which he had been put was removed, and his right leg put in traction, with all the acute suffering that can entail. By the end of the first week in January 1957, Baba was sitting up in bed for a few minutes at a time and taking more solid food. At the request of his advisers, however, and in view of the slow progress he was making and the continued pain, a famous London orthopaedic surgeon was consulted, X-rays of the hip being flown over for him to examine. He had treated Baba previously and now said he would be willing to postpone all other work and fly out to India to perform a particular operation, which he said was essential if Baba were ever to recover completely and be able to walk naturally. Baba sent his thanks but refused the operation, and it was accepted by those about him that he refused because his suffering formed an essential accompaniment to his inner work. "The accident has been a blessing for the universe," he said one evening when the pain was bad, "and a curse for Baba."

York, Dr Harry Kenmore, arrived and began to give Baba treatment, with which Baba said he was very pleased: "He has done his best with satisfactory results." Late in November Baba stated that the sahavas, for which his followers all over the world had been hoping, were to be held, first for the Easterners at Meherabad in February 1958, and for the Westerners at Myrtle Beach in May. To them Baba sent the following message:

My suffering is daily becoming more intense, and my health is daily getting worse, but my physical body continues to bear the burden. Despite it I shall hold the sahavas—I expect from you a deep understanding of my self-imposed suffering, begotten of compassion and love for mankind. Also understand, therefore, that I shall not undergo medical examinations or treatments for my injured hip either in America or Australia. No doctor or treatment will be of any help before the pain I am undergoing has served its purpose.

These sahavas will be unique in the sense that you will witness and share my present universal suffering by being near me as my fortunate companions—being with the Ancient One, who will be completely on the human level with you. . . .

I may give you more, much more, than you expect—or maybe nothing, and that nothing may prove to be everything. So I say, come with open hearts to receive much or nothing from your Divine Beloved. Come prepared to receive not so much of my words but of my Silence.

For the Eastern sahavas devotees were organised into two groups according to language; more than 1,500 in all attended. One devotee from Hamirpur in Northern India, where there existed a long tradition of devotion to Baba, walked the entire distance of more than 1,000 miles, over mountains and rivers and through jungles, taking forty days. The scene when the sahavas ended was something that could happen only in India.

Meherabad is about six miles from the nearest railway station. But with the help of a high official, who was also a devotee, it was arranged that a special train should stop on the track at Meherabad for the departure of each group. "There were streamers of little Baba-flags (of seven colours) round the engine, and a big one hoisted in front. Outside some of the compartments were pasted pictures of Baba, and there were also banners with the words:

> Avatar Meher Baba
>   Is the Soul of souls,
>   The Beloved of the gods,
>   The Life of his lovers
>   And the Slave of his dear ones.*

* The account is condensed from Mani's letter of the 4th March, 1958.

When the train was full, Baba's car was driven down so that he could wave good-bye. "Immediately there rose tremendous cheers of 'Baba! Baba! Avatar Meher Baba Ki Jai!' from every compartment, and when it was obvious they were all intending to leave the train to surge towards Baba's car, He waved a hand and gestured they should not come down.... Baba acknowledged the salute of the engine-driver and gestured that he should start the train. After a very long piercing whistle the 'Baba-train' moved forward, and as the long line of packed compartments filed past Beloved's car, the air thundered with reverberating cries of 'Avatar Meher Baba Ki Jai'. Many were standing on the running boards, the rest leaning way out of the windows till we thought some would surely fall out; some hands folded reverently, hundreds of others waving ecstatically. Baba acknowledged their love with joined hands, or waved and gestured 'I am happy; take me with you'."

Three months later the Western sahavas were held at Myrtle Beach in South Carolina. Two hundred and twenty-five men and women assembled from all over the U.S. and Mexico, from France, Switzerland, Israel and Britain. These sahavas took a dramatic course. On the first full day Baba faced the assembled followers with a straight demand for acceptance of himself as Avatar and the obedience which must follow such acceptance.

"What I want is love and obedience.... Discourses and messages are good, but are mere words.... In the spiritual path there is no room for compromise. Raise your hands who cannot obey me." None raised a hand. "Now raise your hands all who will *try* to obey me." All hands were raised.

In spiritual matters the compromise most acceptable to Western minds is to regard the Master as a saint or unusually holy man. Once planted in this convenient niche and suitably labelled, he can be left to go on being holy, while the disciple feels no obligation either to act on his instructions or refute his claims. But Baba would have none of this.

"I am not a saint. I am the Ancient One; and I tell you, the time has come. When I drop my body, I shall remain in all who love me. I can never die. Love me, obey me, and you will find me."

After listing different types of obedience, leading up to "a fifth obedience which is very rare, absolute obedience, in which light becomes dark* and dark becomes light because the Master says so", Baba went on: "It is impossible to obey me one hundred per cent unless you have one hundred per cent love for me and accept me one hundred per cent as God incarnate. So it is for you who have raised your hands to do my will. The purpose of my coming to the West has been accomplished. Tomorrow we will start discourses. Now let us have some jokes."

But tomorrow they did not start discourses, and on the day following when they met again, it was to hear from Baba that he was thinking of cutting the sahavas short, cancelling a proposed visit to Australia afterwards and flying straight back to India. Faced with the consternation of the company who had made plans to stay here for three weeks, Baba reminded them that only the day before yesterday they had all raised hands signifying obedience—and now his first instruction was to remain happy, whether his stay among them was cut short or not. He told them not to think about their homes and worldly interests, but to concentrate on Baba, and he reminded them of the words of his favourite poet Hafiz: "To be with a Perfect Master for one moment is equal to a hundred years of sincere prayer with all one's heart and soul." A reading was then given.

"I am the Ocean of Love. Draw as much of this love as possible. Make the most of this opportunity. It rests with you to draw as much love as you can out of the Ocean. It does not rest with me to explain to you how you should love me. Does a husband or a wife explain to one another how to love? One thing is certain; I want to give you my love. It depends on each of you to receive it." He further instructed everyone to get a good night's rest before attending since "... if you remain drowsy in my presence you will miss me and your drowsiness will oblige you to remain absent from my presence in spite of your daily attendance."

Understanding the bias of modern man who wants everything on the intellectual plane, to be apprehended, chewed over, discussed, Baba stressed that his sahavas were not some sort of seminar or study course: "Sahavas is the intimacy of give and take between the lovers and the Beloved. There is no need to explain this give and take, for to create an atmosphere of explanations and discourses is to mar the dignity of love which is established only in the closest intimacy.... Take fullest

---

* Note: "becomes dark"; not simply that the disciple accepts the Master's statement without dissent.

advantage of this opportunity in the living presence of the Avatar. Forget everything else but my sahavas and concentrate all your attention on me. I am the Ancient One."

Through the parable of a pet lion, Baba summed up the need for an absolute surrender to God.

> My lovers may be likened to one who is fond of lions and admires them so much that he keeps a lion in his own home. But being afraid of the lion he puts him in a cage. The lion is always encaged; even while he feeds the lion, he feeds the pet animal from a distance and from outside the cage. Baba is treated like the lion by the lovers. There is love; there is admiration; there is an intense desire to see Baba comfortable and happy; and Baba is also frequently fed by love of the lovers. But all this is done, keeping Baba segregated from one's own self. What is wanted of the lovers is that they should open the cage and, through intense love, throw themselves inside the cage to become food for the lion of love. The lover should permit himself to be totally consumed through his own love for the Beloved.

What stands in the lover's way? The intellect, the sense of personal identity, fear to merge and to surrender. So the lover takes refuge in mentalisation, in discussion, but ... "In spite of all explanations and reading of books, words remain mere words. They do not take one any further than intellectual satisfaction. Only love for God works the miracle, because love is beyond mind and reason. What then is the necessity to read?"

Despite his suggestion of an early departure, Baba, as often, had regard to the general wish and remained till the end of the month, making his stay one of fourteen instead of eighteen days, and going on afterwards to Australia for another three. And despite his rejection of discourses and explanations, he allowed discourses to be given and discussions to take place, though he said "... when it comes to giving explanations, I feel like one who climbs a hill and becomes breathless. Giving you discourses and explanations is burdensome to me; and as discussions, discourses and explanations are also included in the affairs of the universe, the whole affair becomes more of a burden to me than ever. Playing marbles, *gilli-danda*, cricket and flying kites are also included in the affairs of the universe; but these unburden the burden. It is like coming down a hill: it is more of a relaxation than exertion. Jokes and humour are also the things which give me relaxation."

Throughout all discourses and explanations, Baba stressed only one theme—obedience and love. And when someone was introduced to Baba with all his qualifications enumerated as is the American custom, Baba replied: "I am unmindful of these qualifications. The only qualification I want you to have is love. I see whether one loves me or not," adding with that childlike directness which took away the pain of a rebuke, "You love me and I am pleased with you."

To most Westerners man is associated with intellect and action, woman with intuition and feeling. Several times during the sahavas Baba emphasised the importance of woman's role, which was symbolised throughout his life by the special position he always gave to Mehera and the women mandali. Here too he made use of a parable.

God is One. He is both father and mother in One. He is in everyone and in everything; but God is beyond this too. I will tell you about God in the Beyond state. In the Beyond State God is both God the father and God the mother simultaneously.

Now we will discuss the worldly father and mother. Suppose a couple have seven sons. It is natural for the father to love those sons who are useful to him, who are healthy, intelligent, brilliant.... Now the six sons of this worldly father are healthy, strong, intelligent and good in all respects; the seventh son is a disabled weakling, innocent, simple and guileless. The father has no love for this seventh son and loves only his six sons. But the mother loves her seventh son the most because he is weak, sick, disabled, simple and guileless.

God is both the father and the mother in One. The Avatars are Sons of the Father in the Beyond state. All past Avataric periods witnessed the presence of the Avatar as the healthy, bright, wise son of God. All this means that the Avatar always remained the Beloved Son of the Father. Note that the Avatar always takes a male form and mingles with mankind as man.

Hitherto, God in the Beyond state did not have occasion to play the part of God the Mother. In this Avataric period, God the Father is very pleased with me at my being infinitely

bright, wise, efficient and perfect in all respects [*Ustad* or
'shrewd'] as my Father wants me to be, and I am the beloved
Son of my Father. At the same time, in this form I am physically disabled. In America, in 1952, I was injured on the left*
side of my physical frame from leg to face. In India, in 1956,
I injured my right side from the head down to the leg. Besides
being physically disabled, I am also infinitely simple and guileless. Thus, I am also the well-beloved Son of my God the
Mother. So in this incarnation, God has the occasion, as it
were, to play the part of both Father and Mother.

Later, possibly in answer to queries as to "how are we to love
you?" from some of his listeners, Baba told a story stressing the
same theme of the need to love and woman's special capacity
for loving.

Have you all heard of Saint Mira?... Mira was a very beautiful girl who lived 200 or 300 years ago. She was the wife of a
royal prince of a wealthy family in North India, who later
became king. She loved Krishna with all her heart, but did not
live at the time of Krishna, about 5,000 years earlier. Her
husband did not like the way she was going about on the
streets for she was the queen and queens did not mix with the
crowd. She would enter the huts of the poor, the name of
Krishna on her lips as she sang. She suffered many trials and
threats to test her love for Krishna; she was locked up in a
room, her food was poisoned, a cobra was concealed in a
bouquet of flowers; she accepted all as a gift of her Lord
Krishna and nothing happened, he protected her. Finally the
king drove her away. She said, 'If the king drives me out I have
a place, but if the Lord of the Universe is displeased, I have
no place.' The people turned against her. As years passed, she
looked radiant in her rags. Then the king came and fell at her
feet. For a man in India to bow down to a woman is a sin,
and to his wife, unforgivable. Yet he fell at her feet because
she was sincere. When she died, all revered her, and now
people repeat her *bhajans* [devotional songs].

I am Krishna, I want all of you to love me as Mira loved
me.

---

* Analytically, the left is regarded as the female side, the right as
masculine.

Two or three days later Baba left for Australia, where under the direction of Francis Brabazon, the Australian poet who had been for years one of his mandali, a centre had been constructed. Baba remained with his Australian followers for three days, and then flew back to India.

It was his last visit to the Western world, and this was the last time most of his Western followers would ever see him.

Chapter 14

THE LONG SECLUSION

DURING THE TWELVE months following the 1958 sahavas Baba withdrew more and more from outward contact. His recent visits to the West were the last, he said, that he would make, and he warned all his followers to expect no more discourses, interviews or gatherings. Even correspondence was not allowed except as a cable in an emergency. Baba spoke often of a coming crisis and the breaking of his silence which would ensue: "On my own I shall not break my silence. Universal crisis will make me do so."

At the beginning of March 1959, Baba went for one week to Bombay where he paid visits to a school and an industrial home for the blind. Though he said nothing to indicate this at the time, these were almost the last such visits he would make. For the next ten years his outward life would be lived in only two places, not more than 70 or 80 miles apart—Meherazad, the cluster of buildings in a garden setting a few miles north of the small town of Ahmednagar, which had been his principal 'home' since 1944, and Guruprasad, an ornamental bungalow on the outskirts of Poona up in the hills, to which Baba and the mandali moved every year for three months from April to June. Guruprasad belonged to a devoted follower, the Maharanee of Baroda, who kept the house with its acres of grounds and gardens available so that Baba could avoid the extreme heat of the plains in summer.

At first Baba used the visits to Guruprasad to allow breaks in his seclusion, and to continue those special receptions for the poor, the outcast and suffering which he had maintained for the past forty years. As knowledge of Baba spread slowly over the continent a tremendous pressure was building up among those who wished to see and touch him, and to derive benefit, spiritual or material, from being in his presence. In May and June 1960, Baba gave darshan to crowds estimated at more than 10,000 in one day, assembling from all parts of India. During

June also there were two of these receptions for the poor to which he always brought a special intensity of love. The description which follows is taken from the 'Family Letters' written by Baba's sister Mani (Manija Sheriar Irani). These letters, sent out every two or three months to Western followers, form the only connected record for the last ten years of Baba's life on earth.

At this Poona program, 160 poor people, both men and women, each received Rs.5 from Baba's hand after He had placed His head on the feet of each one.... Baba sat in a chair before an old table with improvised steps that served as a platform. Each one climbed on to this, and stood before Baba for Him to bow down, while his recipient was strictly instructed not to express thanks or reverence by word or gesture. To have seen Baba place His forehead on these unshod, dusty (and often gnarled and horny) pairs of feet, is not only a deeply moving emotion of the moment, but a never to be forgotten experience.

The Ahmednagar program* was for 150 very poor people, mostly lepers (many of them in a highly advanced state of malignancy), each receiving Rs.5 and a piece of cloth from Baba after He had washed their feet with loving care and touched their feet with His forehead. Eruch tells us this program took nearly two hours, and the exertion left Baba drenched in perspiration.... While the *prasad* of money is an unfailingly welcome relief, in the case of the lepers it seemed overshadowed by their touching incredulity and happiness at Baba's expression of love for them, these usually shunned and 'untouchable' children of God.

From Meherazad, at the end of June, Baba sent out a message to his followers reinforcing the warnings already given:

I want you to remain undisturbed and unshaken by the force of life's currents, for whatever the circumstances they too will be of my own creation.

I want you to remain absorbed as much as possible in thinking of me during my seclusion of six months, when

---

* This took place one week later, after the return from Guruprasad to Meherazad.

circumstances ... will try to drift you away from me. This is the reason why I have repeatedly stressed, while at Guruprasad, that the time has come when I want you all to cling to my *daaman* with both hands—in case the grip of one hand is lost, your other* will serve in good stead.

And lastly, I want you all to remember not to disturb me in any way during my seclusion, not even by writing to me to acknowledge this or to reaffirm your love for me.

All his life, from the moment when he first became conscious of his Avatarhood, Baba had made a practice of retiring into seclusion. But now his seclusion appeared unusually intense even to those who had been with him from the earliest days. At the end of 1960 Eruch wrote in a letter ... "Beloved Baba seems now to be interested in being totally disinterested! He appears to be very absorbed in something very serious and, alone with His unique Silence, He has obviously silenced all activities immediately around Him. He does not want to hear anything and He does not want to see to anything, nor take part in the usual conversation we hold while we sit near Him. ... The atmosphere around Meherazad is charged with a sort of 'stillness'—not inactivity (far from it!) but a sort of HUSH personified."

This deep seclusion was prolonged, with only an occasional brief interlude, until November 1962. At the start of that month he gave for four days the last darshan for lovers from all over the world. This was at Guruprasad to which Baba returned especially for this purpose. Westerners were present in the mornings, Easterners in the afternoons; just under 140 came from America, Europe, Australia, New Zealand, and about 3,000 from all over India, Persia and Pakistan, special platforms and canopies having been erected in the grounds to accommodate so many.

The period at which this darshan took place was one of extreme political crisis. China, having absorbed Tibet—regarded for centuries as the world's 'spiritual power-house'—had launched her armies against India, so that the country was then actually at war. On the far side of the world the two supreme powers, the U.S.A. and the U.S.S.R., which had been squaring up to one

---

* *Daaman* is literally the hem of the garment. And if the right hand is thought of as masculine intellect and reason, which may be argued or ridiculed out of its convictions, the left can represent our feminine aspect of perception, intuition, faith.

another ever since the end of the Second World War, seemed about to come to final grips over the setting-up in Cuba of the Russian missile bases. This must have been in the minds of all those present as Baba's message of welcome was read out.

> My dear Children, Your coming from different places and across oceans has pleased me. And although no sacrifice to be near me is too great, I am touched by the sacrifice that some of you have made.... It is a coming together of children of East and West in the house of their Father.
> All religions of the world proclaim that there is but one God, the Father of all in creation. I am that Father.
> I have come to remind all people that they should live on earth as the children of the one Father until my Grace awakens them to the realisation ... that all divisions and conflicts and hatred are but a shadow play of their own ignorance.
> Although all are my children they ignore the simplicity and beauty of this Truth by indulging in hatreds, conflicts and wars that divide them in enmity, instead of living as one family in their Father's house.... It is time that they become aware of the presence of their Father in their midst and of their responsibility towards Him and themselves....

In a series of profound messages Baba spoke of the nature of creation, with its millions of galaxies. In some, life forms are developed, and in certain planets evolution is completed and human beings exist. But he went on to stress the unique importance of our own planet: "Only on this earth can God be realised. It is not possible for men to contact the worlds that contain the kingdoms of evolutions that are without spiritual development. On these other worlds there are beings that have more intelligence than exists in men. The earth is the centre of creation because men are made in God's image, and only human beings on earth are capable of advancement." Baba ended with the dry comment: "Through your learning the simplest things have been made very difficult."

C. B. Purdom, who had not seen Baba for more than four years, was struck by his changed appearance. "His expression was as bright, his eyes as keen as ever, and his alertness seemed not to have diminished, but he was withdrawn, and for much of the time looked far away, as though not belonging to the world. He constantly smiled and was ready to joke, and his humour had not deserted him, but there was a certain indifference that I had not noticed before. Above all there was an immense sadness that moved me strangely. When he walked one saw that he went heavily."*

Two days later Baba gave those present a stern rebuke, which might also have been directed towards the world in general:

> I had to give you a message on Thursday because you expected one; and the theme of the message was on your being my children, because despite much talk about a Baba-family there is more a semblance than a reality of kinship among you who are the children of One Father.
>
> True children of One Father do not greet one another with smiles and embraces and at the same time harbour grudges and ill-feeling, but have an active concern in their hearts for the well-being of one another and make sacrifices for that well-being.
>
> If you make me your real Father, all differences and contentions between you, and all personal problems in connection with your lives, will become dissolved in the Ocean of my Love....
>
> Unless there is a brotherly feeling in your hearts, all the words that you speak or print in my name are hollow; all the miles that you travel in my cause are zero; all organisations for my work are but an appearance of activity; all buildings to contain me are empty places and all statues that you make to embody me are of someone else.
>
> I have been patient and indulgent... because you have been very young children in my love, and children must have some sort of games to play. But now you are older and are beginning to realise that there is a greater work ahead of you than what you have been doing. And you have been searching your minds and hearts as to what this work might be.
>
> It is not a different work... it is the same work done in a different way. And that way is the way of effacement, which means the more you work for me the less important you feel in yourself. You must always remember that I alone do my work... I allow you to work for me so that you have the opportunity to use your talent and capacities selflessly and so draw closer to me....
>
> When you put my work before yourself the work will go

* *The God-Man*, p. 361.

right, though not necessarily smoothly. And when the work does not go right it means you have put yourself between it and its accomplishment.

The way of my work is the way of effacement, which is the way of strength, not of weakness, and through it you become mature in my love. . . .

Towards the close of the gathering a newspaperman asked Baba about the situation in the war with China, and what its outcome would be. "As I am the Ancient One and as I am in India," Baba answered, "in the final outcome India will be victorious." This was reported next day all over the country, omitting everything except the last four words.

Before the darshan ended Baba permitted the mandali to bow down before him one by one. It was the first time for twenty-two years that he had allowed this, and it seemed to signify an even deeper withdrawal in which the breaks would be fewer and briefer still. From time to time during his annual stay at Guruprasad there would be 'song feasts' in which famous Indian singers took part and visitors would be allowed to come, especially on Sunday afternoons. At times too the visitors would themselves put on plays and entertainments for him. Two and a half years later in May 1965, there were eight days of further darshan for the Eastern followers, some of whom travelled great distances to be present—one group from Iran spending no fewer than eleven days on their laborious train journey. For the end of the same year corresponding sahavas were projected for the Westerners, but before December came they were postponed, and continued to be put off year after year as Baba's seclusion was extended. This seclusion was the opposite of retirement. It was not a withdrawal from work but a withdrawal into work.

What the true nature of this work might be, even those whose lives were spent in Baba's company knew little. All they gleaned from a rare comment was, first, that it went on unceasingly. "You see me doing all this," Baba told them once during an interlude at Guruprasad in June 1963, "but simultaneously my work continues. It is as breathing is to you—you talk, work, play, eat, sleep etc., but you never stop breathing. It is the same with my work, which continues without a stop whatever else I may appear to be doing."

Secondly, they understood that it was directly related to the world situation at any given moment and carried out 'on the

THE LONG SECLUSION

inner planes', invisibly and imperceptibly, in the way that Baba worked on the minds of audiences absorbed in some entertainment.

Thirdly, they could see for themselves that it involved intense suffering both bodily and mental. "After I return to Meherazad," he said in the summer of 1963, "there will be an increase in suffering and chaos the world over. It will be a reflection of the suffering I will undergo during the nine months."

This was said shortly before Baba began his last, seemingly unending—indeed literally unending though not quite unbroken —seclusion, which would continue for longer than five years. And if for the world as a whole these years were ones of "suffering and chaos", including the horrors of the Vietnam war, the assassination of the American president, the Six-Day war in Israel, with the spate of hi-jackings and killings which have followed, for India this has been particularly true. The country has had to face war, natural disasters of flood with crop failure on a gigantic scale, famine and the death of two leaders, Nehru and Shastri.

At first Baba's physical pain centred round the hip joint which had been injured in the crash and which he steadfastly refused to have operated on. "The pain is bad, but the extent of my work being done is good." As years went by, and with the help of the blind chiropractor, Dr Harry Kenmore, this was much eased, but now there came a new cause of suffering, whose physical cause may have been displacement resulting from the original hip injury. In a letter of April 1965, Mani wrote: "Besides the continuous pain in His hip-joint and His inability to walk freely, He has had since the last many months pain in the cervical spine, i.e. in the nape of the neck and extending down the shoulders. Of late the pain has become intense.... When, on one of his recurrent visits to Meherazad, Dr Ginde expressed his distress and surprise at the stubbornness of the pain, Beloved Baba patted him lovingly on the arm and said, 'Don't worry. It is all My will. I alone know the cause of my pain, and it will go away after July. All the same I want you to go on doing your best to lessen it,' (adding after a while) 'and I will do my best to increase it!' ... Baba has told the mandali more than once, 'It is but the [yoke of] universal suffering round my neck'—and indeed the surgical collar that He wears seems to us painfully symbolical of this fact."

Five months later, announcing the cancellation of the Western sahavas planned for December, Baba said: "The world situation is very bad, and growing worse daily. The pressure of my universal work is affecting my health tremendously, and the pain in my neck is beyond limit."

Not all the record of these years is one of suffering, however. There are glimpses of Baba, seated on a high stool because movement was painful, playing table tennis with the mandali, or out in the garden enjoying a game called 'Seven Tiles', in which the driver and gardeners took part as well. In this Indian version of skittles or bowls, seven pieces of stone or tile are balanced on top of each other, and the player tries to knock them all down with a ball. Baba took great pleasure in the gardens, in watching the animals and birds both tame and wild. He enjoyed listening to music: "Teatime at Meherazad," wrote Mani, "is a happy hour for us women, when we sit together at the dining table with the Beloved; and mingling with snatches of conversation and the tinkle of teaspoons in cups, is the music from our transistor radio.... This would find Baba drumming briskly on the table in rhythm with the music, the response from our brass tea-kettle being a jerky little dance as it would bob up and down with the vibration of the table."

Children and child-like people afforded him relief. He responded instantly to the loving acceptance of children, who had no requests to make, were not interested in hearing discourses, but wanted only to get as close to him as they could. At Guruprasad in an assembly so crowded that there seemed no inch of floor space left, Baba singled out and silently beckoned to him a little girl hardly four years old. She made her way forward, bowed solemnly before him, and then smiled ecstatically as Baba drew her to him, embraced her and caressed her cheeks. She had come, it was later learned, from a place a long way from Poona. Her parents were not with her. Hearing that some neighbours were travelling to Poona to see Baba, she had urged and insisted with tears that her mother allow her to go with them and see him.

In another crowded gathering during the same stay, there was a mother having trouble with two boisterous children. No one supposed that Baba had even noticed her, occupied as he was with receiving a long line of visitors and being garlanded. But when the woman finally reached Baba, he asked: "Do these kids trouble you?"

"Yes, Baba, indeed they do!" she answered feelingly.

"If only two children can make your life a hell," Baba asked her, "can you imagine my plight who has billions of children?"

One of the mandali whose company Baba specially enjoyed was Kaka, a companion from the earliest days who had travelled several times with Baba to the West, and taken part in many 'mast hunts'. At Meherazad he acted as manager, and it was he who had originally given the place its name. Totally unselfconscious, Kaka would join in any entertainment and often provided one himself by his unique use of language. "Waddling beside Baba like a protective hen" he would keep up a running fire of observation and comment. Undaunted by a memory which faltered as he aged, Kaka would make up any words he found himself short of, and drop in alternative expressions which resembled those he was trying to recall. Of Kaka, Baba said: "While everybody adds to my burden, Kaka removes a fraction of it."

Just occasionally too the pain would lift, and in June 1967, Mani reported happily from Guruprasad: "Each morning and afternoon we have seen the Beloved striding the length of the marble-tiled verandah, to and from the mandali's hall. Added to our joy at seeing Him walk like this is seeing the pleasure it gives Him, when at the end of a stride He may ask with a delighted smile 'How do I walk?'"

In general, however, the record of these years is one of unending work and increasing pain. Of the pain in his neck Dr Ram Ginde, a leading neuro-surgeon from Bombay who was also a devoted follower, wrote to Dr Goher, a member of the mandali and Baba's personal physician: "Whatever I know from the knowledge of His cervical condition, I have tried to do in all sincerity. But I must admit...my utter failure in regard to relieving Beloved Baba's pain. I plead quite helpless in treating Him who is as powerful as, nay more powerful than, an ocean and as helpless as a kitten at one and the same time."

Not surprisingly, as they puzzled over this mysterious pain, those around Baba recalled that back in 1940, Chatti Baba—one of the greatest of masts, then living at Meherabad with Baba—had said that all suffering borne by Baba arose out of his compassion and love for humanity. The suffering yet to come upon the earth was so great that it would not be able to sustain the burden, and so Baba would take one end of the yoke upon his own shoulder.

In a message sent out on 1st March, 1968, postponing the end of his seclusion once again until the 21st May, Baba wrote: "None can have the least idea of the immensity of the work I am doing in this seclusion. The only hint I can give is that, compared with the work I do in seclusion, all the important work of the world put together is completely insignificant. Although for me the burden of the work is crushing, the result of my work will be intensely felt by all people in the world."

But Baba's seclusion did not end in May, any more than it had ended in March, or in February, or in November. He continued his work throughout his yearly visit to Guruprasad and on through the month of July after his return.

At last, on the evening of Tuesday, 30th July, 1968, he declared: "My work is done. It is completed one hundred per cent to my satisfaction. The result of this work will also be one hundred per cent and will manifest from the end of September."

Chapter 15

THE LAST SAHAVAS

WHEN BABA EMERGED from that last long-sustained seclusion, it was with his physical nature almost at breaking-point. To a few specially summoned to Meherabad in October 1968, he said: "No doubt you people and my lovers everywhere have been wondering why, when my period of intense work in seclusion has finished, I have still not allowed my lovers to see me.

"The strain of that eighteen months' work was tremendous. I used to sit alone in my room for some hours each day while complete silence was imposed on the mandali.... The strain was not in the work itself, although I was working on all planes of consciousness, but in keeping my link with the gross plane. To keep this link I had to continuously hammer my right thigh with my fist... it will yet take some time for all traces of the strain to disappear." Baba went on to announce the news all were eagerly awaiting: a great gathering was to be held in Guruprasad for both Easterners and Westerners. It was to last for a fixed number of hours each day from the 10th April to the 10th June, 1969. As always, the most careful preparations had been put in train with detailed instructions for all who would attend—not forgetting a message of comfort for those wishing to come but unable to do so.

Some of those hearing the announcement were apprehensive as to whether Baba's body could endure the strain of such an arduous programme, but he reassured them: "It will be easy for me to give my lovers my darshan, so you are not to feel concerned about it. I will give darshan reclining and that will be no strain on my body. It will be different from all previous darshans and it will be the last in silence. Although I will be reclining I will be very strong. My physical condition now is because of my work, but by then my work will be complete and my exultation will be great...."

Mani's letter carrying the news of the forthcoming sahavas overseas ended with Baba's words:

"I have been saying: the Time is near,
it is fast approaching, it is close at hand.
Today I say: *the Time has come.* Remember this!"

Though Baba had appeared to make light of anxiety over his health, those about him felt growing apprehension, especially when from the beginning of December he began to suffer muscular spasms. A blood check was called for, and the doctors simply could not believe what it showed. They called for a second, which confirmed the first. Dr Ginde, who was summoned from Bombay, later recalled: "I saw Beloved Baba again on 19th December, 1968, as by then His health had deteriorated further. Beloved Baba had become pale due to anaemia, there was swelling around His feet and ankles. He was unable to sit up. He was getting spasms of His limbs. . . ."*

On the 22nd December, Mehera's birthday was celebrated as it had always been, and on the following day Baba took part in the wedding of his nephew Dara, son of his younger brother Adi S. Irani who had come over from England with his wife and daughter. From the 26th December the spasms increased, and Baba repeatedly told the mandali, "The time is very near." On 9th January, 1969, when Franee, Adi's wife, came to see him before going back to England, Baba told her not to worry about his health, since "All will be well by the end of this month."

Up till the 12th January, Baba was still going over every morning and afternoon to the room occupied by the men mandali, as had long been his custom. But after this day he never left his own room. On the 30th January the spasms became far worse. Several persons had to be in attendance day and night, and would hold tightly on to his legs when a spasm shook his body. The pain was extreme. At 9.30 that night Baba told Bhau Kalchuri, one of his mandali, who had been doing night duty for him for many years, "I am not this body." At 3.45 a.m. the mandali were summoned, and groups of men and women remained in constant attendance throughout the rest of the night and the following morning. At one point in the morning Baba sent over to the mandali's room for a board on which were written up three couplets from his favourite poet Hafiz. They

* This and much else in this chapter is taken from *Meher Baba's Last Sahavas* by Dr H. P. Bharucha, published by himself from Navsari, Gujarat, India.

were ones he had quoted many times, and it was as if he wished to imprint them finally upon their memories.

I am the slave of the Master who has released me from ignorance; whatever my Master does is of the highest benefit to all concerned.

Befitting a fortunate slave, carry out every command of the Master without any question of 'why' and 'what'.

About what you hear from the Master, never say it is wrong, because, my dear, the fault lies in your own incapacity to understand Him.

Baba enquired a number of times for Dr Ginde, who had been summoned from Bombay, making the gesture of tracing out a 'G'. The least movement could precipitate a spasm and each time he would wince at the pain; he had developed another severe pain in his back. To relieve the spasms Padri was giving Baba pills which had to be administered every ten minutes. Padri gave Baba the fourth dose at 12.0 noon, and Baba for the last time enquired whether Dr Ginde had yet come. Hearing he had not, Baba gestured, "It is getting late."

At 12.15 p.m. Baba was seized with an exceedingly severe spasm. "He was sitting on His surgical bed with His back and head raised.* Baba flexed His arms and closed His mouth tightly. His respiration suddenly stopped. There was no relaxation after the spasm and Baba became motionless. Eruch, using his wits, tried to open Baba's mouth. He found that the tongue had fallen back. Eruch put his mouth on Baba's mouth and began to breathe into his lungs forcibly. This mouth to mouth resuscitation was carried on for nearly thirty minutes. Francis and Bhau relieved him for a short while. Adi was immediately phoned to bring Dr Brieseman and an oxygen cylinder from the Mission hospital at Ahmednagar. Pendu kept his hand on Baba's pulse. Dr Goher was busy giving several injections in an attempt to revive Baba.

"At about 12.40 p.m., Dr Ginde arrived followed by Adi and Dr Brieseman. They brought an oxygen cylinder with them. Eruch had collapsed on the floor out of sheer exhaustion. Dr Brieseman gave a cardiac massage. He then checked Baba's

* Quoted verbatim from *Meher Baba's Last Sahavas*.

heart with a stethoscope and passed it on to Dr Donkin, who, after examining Baba, gave it to Dr Ginde. The three doctors discussed something which the mandali did not understand. Dr Ginde checked Baba's eye reflexes. The heart had stopped, the reflexes were gone and life was extinct!"

And now it became clear why Baba had been so insistent on Dr Ginde's arrival. The women mandali were distracted; they could not believe Baba had laid down his body and thought he must be in a coma or a trance. Among the men "all minds seemed to have come to a standstill". Dr Ginde thereupon took charge. He told them they must not be emotional but practical, and himself wrote out Baba's death certificate. As they were discussing how to act, Eruch recalled Baba's having told him more than once, "Whenever my body drops, bring me and put me in the crypt at Meherabad." Dr Ginde said that if this was to be done, the removal should be carried out within six hours, and on learning that the crypt floor was of stone, he said that the stones would have to be taken up. Padri was charged with the task, went over to Meherabad, and got to work. It was the noise of Padri's digging which first warned the villagers of Arangaon that something was amiss. Meantime Chhagan, another of the mandali, had been sent to Ahmednagar to have a wooden board prepared on which Baba's body could be laid, together with a cover for the coffin in which later it would be interred.

Baba's body was now lifted on to a stretcher and laid on his aluminium bed, and the men of the mandali came one by one to bow down to their Master for the last time in the place which had been his home and theirs for more than twenty years. Late in the afternoon an ambulance arrived to carry Baba's body to the Tomb at Meherabad. As the ambulance crept slowly up the hill, the Arangaon villagers, already alerted by the noise of digging, guessed what had happened, and the news spread rapidly.

Of the Meherabad hill Baba had once said: "The major portion of my Universal work was done on this hill. I have selected this spot for my last resting-place; when I drop the body, it shall rest here, in my Tomb. I have fasted here for six months. I used to lie down here in the crypt taking only water and coffee. ... After I drop my body the physical remains will rest here, and this hill will become an important place of pilgrimage for the world. After seventy years ... a big township will grow around here."

Lifted from the ambulance, Baba's body was placed in a cabin opposite the Tomb door. Then after Padri had announced that the floor was dug and the Tomb all in order, the stretcher was carried from the cabin to the entrance and laid on the wooden board brought by Chhagan. Under one end Eruch had put three stone slabs from the floor, and now a pillow was placed beneath Baba's head. A scarf, which had already been tied round his head and chin, was rearranged. Baba lay now with his head to the north and his eyes closed, facing the steps by which his followers would descend into the crypt. Some time before this, Baba had asked the mandali whether it would be all right if he gave the forthcoming darshan lying down. They supposed he was referring to his state of health which might prevent his sitting up for the whole period, and agreed. Thereupon Baba had asked them to raise his head so that his lovers could see him from a distance. Only now did they realise his meaning.

Almost immediately after Baba laid down his body, the men mandali had discussed the message to be sent out to the world. Finally they agreed on the wording: "Avatar Meher Baba dropped His physical body at 12.15 p.m. on 31st January, 1969, at Meherazad to live eternally in the hearts of all His lovers. Beloved Baba's body will be interred at Meherabad Arangaon on 1st February at 10.0 a.m. in the Tomb He had ordered to be built long ago."

All afternoon Adi K. Irani, Baba's secretary and lifelong companion, had been cabling this message to Baba centres and lovers in India and abroad. The All-India radio put the news out the same evening, repeating the announcement several times on the following day, sometimes with a brief sketch of Baba's life. Next day the B.B.C. also announced his passing and overseas newspapers carried the news. Throughout the world the reaction of most Baba followers was of disbelief; on being told the news, they supposed that either their informant or the newspaper must be mistaken. The small telegraph office in Ahmednagar was overwhelmed with cables calling for confirmation, denial or fuller information. But from neighbouring districts numbers of followers who had heard the radio simply left everything and set off for Meherabad. Many came without waiting to get leave from work, not stopping to collect clothes or cash or food. They came as on a pilgrimage whose purpose justifies all sacrifice and the cutting through of all convention. By sunrise they were swarming in to Meherabad on foot or bicycle, in ox-carts or horse-drawn vehicles. Special buses had been laid on for the six miles between Ahmednagar and Meherabad. Other devotees who lived farther off and could not reach Meherabad by ten o'clock on the Saturday, the time announced for the interment, sent cables pleading that this be put off until they could arrive.

The time had originally been fixed on medical advice, that since the body had not been embalmed it must be buried within twenty hours. However Mehera and Mani recalled Baba's conveying to them by signs on the last morning that "after seven days he would be one hundred per cent free". They interpreted this as meaning that interment should not take place for seven days, but that his body should be left uncovered, if possible, for the full period. It was in accordance with this decision that Baba's body had been laid in a reclining position, garlanded and covered with flowers regularly renewed, and surrounded by blocks of ice which were changed every few hours. Guarded continually, it was open to all from near and far who sought to pay their final tribute.

And now from early on the morning of Saturday, the 1st February, the crowds were beginning to arrive. They were drawn by the deep Indian conviction that, while it is always blessed to be near the Perfect Master, it is a duty when he lays down his body to express love and devotion by one's presence. Soon every foot of space was occupied by campers. The big hall at lower Meherabad where Baba used to hold meetings and sahavas gatherings was crammed, and the verandahs surrounding it as well. On the railway which cuts Meherabad in two, drivers obliged their passengers by stopping trains in the open to allow them to scramble out. Others whose trains could not stop sounded their whistles in salute.

The mandali and their helpers were concerned to do everything they could for the devotees. A makeshift awning was put up in front of the Tomb to provide shade. No food was available nearer than Ahmednagar so that many, having brought nothing with them, lived on water. But on the next day, Sunday, Chhagan organised the cooking of quantities of rice and vegetables in Ahmednagar and its transport to Meherabad. Before long, too, a small canteen opened up. There is no electricity in Meherabad, but devotees from Andhra set up a generator supplying power for some forty fluorescent lights. At sunset this would

THE LAST SAHAVAS

be turned on to light up the Tomb and the surrounding area which made Meherabad Hill visible in the darkness for miles around. Catching sight of it, passengers in trains and buses would stand up and bow, and trains would sound their whistles. Some of the lights shone on a platform, at one end of which groups of singers from various centres kept up sacred songs and music almost until daylight. Some were reminded of the remark Baba had made years before on returning from a tour in Andhra: "My lovers sang outside my window all night while I rested."

All who came had only one concern—to have a last sight of Baba and to take his darshan. They came bringing flowers and garlands which were collected from them at the door. A continuous flow of people moved up to the entrance, bowed or knelt down, left their flowers, and moved on. Others came inside and bowed. Others again went on down the five steps to touch Baba's feet for the last time. Once inside they were unwilling to leave and had to be asked to make room for other waiting devotees. Some picked up fallen flowers or petals which they would cherish all their lives, or carry back as a blessing for the families they left behind. Two volunteers were continually present in the Tomb, one to keep off flies and mosquitoes with a fan, while the other collected flowers at the door, or swabbed the floor with a wet cloth to keep down dust. For a full week the Tomb was kept open, apart from a short period during two nights. Three times each day the doors were closed for a brief spell while Eruch with a couple of helpers changed the blocks of ice surrounding Baba. For every task there was a rush of volunteers eager to find some way of expressing the love which filled their hearts and could often be seen pouring down their cheeks.

Each day began with prayers in which all took part, and with a report from Dr Goher as to whether the body had yet to be interred. On the eighth day, Friday, 7th February, it was generally known that the sahavas would end and interment take place soon after midday. Newspapers had also announced that this was the final day, and the crowds pouring in had swelled accordingly. It was the week of the full moon, and those in Meherabad had been astir since 3.0 a.m.; by 4.30 all had assembled at the entrance. As it happened, the 7th February was Baba's birthday by the Zoroastrian calendar (25th February by ours), and it had been announced that at 5.0 a.m., his actual birth moment, all should salute him with the cry of 'Avatar

Meher Baba Ki Jai' three times repeated. From 7.0 a.m. no one was allowed inside the Tomb except the two attendants, but so many begged a share of this last task that they were allowed only two minutes of service each.

During that morning as the thousands of devotees, those who had spent the night there and others newly assembled, stood silently round the tomb, their hearts were full of memories of Baba and their minds of his treasured sayings:

Things that are real are always given and received in silence.

I am the One so many seek and so few find. No amount of intellect can fathom me. No amount of austerity can attain me. Only when one loves me and loves one's self in me, am I found.

When I drop my body, I will remain in all who love me. I can never die. Love me, obey me, and you will find me.

There were some Westerners present too, a handful who, on hearing the news, had also left everything and come here. They perhaps remembered others of his sayings:

God is not to be found in the skies or in the caves of the Himalayas. God is in the heart of each one. Once your heart is clean, God will shine out of it.

However far man may fling himself into outer space... man will not change—wherever he goes he will remain what he is. It is when man travels within himself that he experiences a metamorphosis of himself. It is this journeying that matters, for the infinite treasure—God—is within man, and not to be found anywhere outside himself.

At a quarter past midday a threefold cry of 'Avatar Meher Baba Ki Jai' rang out once more. The doors of the Tomb were closed. Mehera and the women mandali entered for the last time as the crowd stood by in total silence. When they left, the men mandali assembled and placed the coffin cover over their beloved Master. The lid was heaped with flowers and earth placed over it. Finally the crypt itself was levelled up with earth. By five o'clock the work was done and the Tomb swept and cleaned.

Most of the lovers had left by now, and as the sun began to sink the last small groups were making their way home. They carried their sorrow with them, but they carried something else as well. For in the words of Dr Bharucha, one of those who had left home the moment he heard the news, "Once an inner contact is established with Baba, the Divine Shepherd folds His sheep with His love, wherever He is, wherever they are, irrespective of time or space."

Those who had lived close to Baba for many years, the men and women mandalis, suffered an intensity of deprivation which made them feel, and possibly sometimes wish, that life itself were ending. Two of them did die very shortly, Kaka within a month and Dr Donkin a few months later. All, living or dying, would echo the words of Mani: "To have what one wants is to have everything. To us, being with Baba was everything—and we had it." Those throughout the world who had made contact with Baba in one way or another turned to their memories with heartfelt gratitude. Those who had made the journey experienced the joy of knowing that all their effort was worth-while since they had been able to pay tribute to their Master at his last sahavas. And those who had failed to make the journey could think over his tender, humorous reminder: "I am in each heart but I am sleeping there. It is my old, old habit. In order to awaken me you should always call out to me, saying 'Baba, Baba, Baba!' Then I, who am in your heart, will not find any pleasure in remaining asleep. Let alone sleep, I shall not find time even to doze!"

Part Two:
His Teaching

INTRODUCTION

LIKE EVERY AVATAR, Meher Baba has left mankind the example of his life. And though he stressed many times that "I have come not to teach but to awaken", he has also left a body of teaching which opens a new chapter in religious thought. Baba's teaching on the nature of the universe is contained largely in the book *God Speaks*. His teaching about human life and its purpose is to be found mainly in his 'Discourses', originally published in India in five volumes between 1938 and 1954.

The late Charles Purdom, one of the earliest and most courageously committed of Baba's followers in Britain, edited an edition for Western readers.* In the course of a moving and discerning introduction, he wrote: "These discourses cover a wide field, but they begin and end with the reader himself. This is therefore a dangerous book. Baba is dangerous, as all who have been near him know—He will not leave alone anyone who listens to him. This therefore is not a book for those who do not wish to be disturbed and who propose to go on living as they have always done. Such readers will not like it. This is not a book for idle reading, but for quiet hours, for solitude, and for those who crave for their lives to be changed."

In the chapters which follow, the authors have tried to convey something of the power and profundity of these Discourses by giving extracts from them on a few particular themes.† Our purpose in doing this is twofold. First, the record of Baba's life would be incomplete without some further impression of his teaching, however sketchy. Secondly, to encourage the reader to go directly to the source and start studying the Discourses himself.

One thing we must make clear. The role of the Avatar is to

---

* *God to Man and Man to God*, the Discourses of Meher Baba with an introduction by C. B. Purdom. Victor Gollancz, 1955.

† These extracts have been taken, with some condensation, from a third edition of the Discourses, edited by Ivy Oneita Duce and Don E. Stevens, and published in three volumes as a paperback in the U.S.A. by Sufism Reoriented Inc. in 1967.

point the way to mankind, and prove by his own life that it is a way which can be followed. The task of the writer is to try, within the limitations of understanding and capacity, to draw attention to what the Avatar has said and done. In doing so he/she cannot escape the charge of indicating to others a road which it is far beyond his or her own powers to travel. The only answer to such a charge must be to admit its truth. But if one should only write of what lies within one's own limits of achievements, no book on such a theme could even be attempted. The sign-post does not claim to have climbed the mountain to which it points the way.

In the following extracts the reader will find that much more than mental effort is demanded of him, he is also faced with a truly heroic programme of spiritual development, to be sustained perhaps over many lives. But one part of the Avatar's achievement is always to raise men's sights. If we take only two of the most familiar sayings of Christ, we can see how immensely more difficult they must have appeared to make life for all who sought to follow him. "Resist not evil: but whosoever shall smite thee on thy right cheek, turn to him the other also." And "Ye have heard that it was said by them of old time, Thou shall not commit adultery: But I say unto you, that whosoever looketh after a woman to lust after her hath committed adultery with her already in his heart." For two thousand years men have recognised the wisdom and justice of these sayings, but few indeed have tried to live by them.

So too the teachings of Baba raise our spiritual sights, and the first impression may well be of the immense difficulty of the road he indicates. "Being the total manifestation of God in human form, he [the Avatar] is like a gauge against which man can measure what he is and what he may become. He trues the standard of human values by interpreting them in terms of divinely human life.... The Avatar awakens contemporary humanity to a realisation of its true spiritual nature, gives liberation to those who are ready, and quickens the life of the spirit in his time.... He has demonstrated the possibility of a divine life for all humanity, of a heavenly life on earth. Those who have the necessary courage and integrity can follow when they will."

Chapter 16

THE DRAMA OF THE EGO

BACK IN 1932, when Meher Baba paid his second visit to England, he gave an interview to the well-known journalist, James Douglas.* During this, Douglas asked Baba: "What is your secret?"

To which Baba replied: "The elimination of the ego."

What did this mysterious sentence mean, and what relevance has it to man's present situation?

If we had to describe that situation in a single word, the one which would seem most apt would probably be 'frustration'. On a material level mankind has never been so united. Every continent, almost every country, is accessible in a few hours to every other. A network of communications, ceaselessly extended and improved, carries the happenings of each day into our homes. The political machinery to unite the world has been established and accepted, and a single language, English, is rapidly becoming almost universal. Yet inwardly man has never been more disunited and despairing; it is as if, having reached the end of some enormous journey, he finds that there is nothing there.

What modern man sees as he looks around the world is almost everywhere the same, the self-indulgence of the few against the hardships and sufferings of the many. And the communications media, which could provide potent means to assert justice and attract relief where they are needed, serve mainly, it seems, to accustom the onlooker to the misery of others, conditioning us into the acceptance of violence, brutality, corruption, not just as part of life but as its dominating factors.

In the Western world, where we choose our political leaders and where much of what they do comes to light before long, ordinary men and women are reaching the conviction that our destinies tend to fall into the hands of men who are actually greedier, more dishonest and less public-spirited than we are ourselves. The best that can be said of them is perhaps that they

* Reported more fully earlier on, in chapter 6.

are very like ourselves, and that though we may not admire or approve them, we deserve them. In the past there existed an Age of Faith and an Age of Reason, once even, it is said, a Golden Age. If we had to give a title to our own, it would be the Age of Cynicism or perhaps the Age of Desperation.

Who is to blame? What has happened to man's hopes and dreams for himself and for a better world? Why—if we can establish the machinery to bring justice and harmony among nations, races, classes—can we not make it work? Is there some ingredient missing from our formula, some mysterious 'X' which if we could only find it, would cause the product to achieve everything claimed on its behalf—so that we all actually started to live as we know we ought to live, not only in peace and fellowship but in conscious happiness? Is it possible that the efforts which are continually made by people of goodwill, to improve the quality of life and the relations between peoples, are applied mainly in the wrong direction—outwards into the world over which we have little or no control, but seldom or never towards altering the only person over whom one has any control, oneself? Is it practicable to alter oneself? How can it be done? And what would the consequences be if one did?

Baba's discourse entitled "The Nature of the Ego and Its Termination" is organised in three parts:

1. The Ego as the Centre of Conflict.
2. The Ego as an Affirmation of Separateness.
3. The Forms of the Ego and Their Dissolution.

Part 1 traces the origin of the ego and explains the function it performs as a stage in man's development. The story begins far back in the record of evolution:

> In the pre-human stage consciousness *has* experiences, but these experiences are not brought into relation with a central 'I'. The dog is angry, but does not continue to feel, 'I am angry.' Even he learns through some experiences and thus bases the action of one experience on another, but this action is a result of a semi-mechanical tension of connected imprints. This is different from the intelligent synthesis of experience which the development of I-consciousness makes possible. The first step in submitting the working of isolated impressions to intelligent regulation consists in bringing them into relation

with the centre of consciousness which appears as the explicit ego....

Human consciousness would have been nothing more than a repository for accumulated imprints of varied experiences, had it not also contained the principle of ego-centred integration, which expresses itself in the attempt to organise and understand experience. The process of understanding experience implies capacity to hold different experiences together as parts of a unity, and the capacity to evaluate them by being brought into mutual relation. The integration of the opposites of experience is a condition of emancipating consciousness from the thraldom of diverse compulsions and repulsions which tend to dominate consciousness irrespective of valuation.... Thus the ego emerges as an explicit and unfailing accompaniment to all the happenings of mental life.... The psychic energy would be caught up endlessly in the multitudinous mazes of experience, frittered away and dissipated were there no *provisional nucleus* to take stock of all acquired experience and bind it together, thus securing a working equilibrium which makes for a planned and organised life.

It is a mistake therefore to imagine that the arising of the ego is without any purpose. Though it arises only to vanish in the end, it fulfils a need which could not have been ignored in the long journey of the soul. The ego is not meant to be a permanent handicap, since it can be transcended and outgrown through spiritual endeavour. Nevertheless, the phase of ego-formation must be looked upon as a *necessary but temporary evil* in the further progress of consciousness.

Having explained how and why the ego comes into existence, Baba goes on to demonstrate how, while striving to establish unity and integration, the ego not only fails to realise such an objective, but also inevitably becomes itself the seat of conflicts.

Since the ego takes shelter in the false idea of being the body, it is a source of much illusion which vitiates experience. It is of the essence of the ego that it should feel separate from the rest of life by contrasting itself with other forms of life. Thus, although inwardly trying to complete and integrate individual experience, the ego also creates an artificial division between external and internal life in the very attempt to feel and secure its own existence. This division in the totality of life cannot but have reverberations in the inner individual life over which the ego presides as a guiding genius.... The incompleteness of its attainment is evident from the internal conflict which is never absent so long as experience is being faced from the ego's point of view.

As a result of this division, "the ego represents a deep and fundamental principle of ignorance" about the true nature of life, leading us into every kind of difficulty and conflict, which the ego always attempts to solve through false valuation and wrong choice, based on what it supposes to be its own interests as against those of other people. The ego is thus the source of competitiveness and self-interest in all its forms. It is impossible for the ego, whose fundamental belief is its own uniqueness and isolation, to accept that all life is one; that we are linked, not only with each other but with creation as a whole, through spirit; that the misery and degradation of some affects the quality of life for all. On the contrary, the ego tends to look on the sufferings and humiliations of others as evidence of its own superiority. And so far from seeing life as a unity, it regards existence as a struggle in which it is advantageous always to come out on top and, acting on this belief, makes life far more of a struggle than it ought to be.

In the world of spirit, the attitude of the ego may be compared to that of prosperous people living complacently among the starving and ill-housed, unaware that the sufferings of their neighbours will produce disease and plague which must inevitably before long reach themselves.

Since the ego's driving-force is invariably self-interest, and since human beings are governed by their egos, it is apparent that no new form of political organisation, no plan for social betterment, no church or religious institution, however lofty its ideals, will ever achieve its aims. Instead of transforming the quality of life, it will itself undergo transformation, or rather decomposition, since the egos of those taking part will before long start using it as a vehicle for their own aggrandisement.*

We can see all this in the outside world, but it is also possible, if one makes the effort to detach oneself and listen intently to one's own pattern of thoughts, actually to hear the ego speaking. In most of us indeed it keeps up a continuous monologue based

---

* This is the underlying theme of George Orwell's famous satire *Animal Farm*.

THE DRAMA OF THE EGO

on the idea of 'I' and 'mine' and centring round the themes 'I want', 'I mean to have' and ... 'in a few years' time when I've got this or that'. Often the tone of this monologue is aggressive, for most egos are touchy and quick to take offence ... 'I'll soon put a stop to that' ... 'they'd better mind their step' ... 'she can't go on treating me like this' ... At other times or in other persons, the voice of the ego is feeble and self-pitying ... 'I've really had as much as I can take' ... 'I don't know why things like this always happen to *me*' ... ' I just don't see how I'm going to cope'. Or else, faced with disappointment and frustration, the ego takes off into boastful fantasies and day-dreams. In these it asserts its superiority and is acclaimed by humiliated rivals, consoling itself by the withdrawal from reality for its own inner emptiness.*

Every thought, emotion, action which springs from the idea of exclusive, separative existence is a manifestation of the ego. All feelings like 'I am someone of such and such a type, someone different and special', and that *my* house, *my* car, *my* clothes are different from other people's; all emotions tending to exclude or reject others—hatred, resentment, fear, greed, jealousy, contempt —fortify and feed the ego. Under its domination we all do actions of which we afterwards say: "I just don't understand how it can have happened", or "I don't know what came over me", as though the action concerned were not our own but the result of some outside person or force which had assumed control. Meantime, through the sense of separation which these negative emotions stir up and maintain, and through the words and acts which are the consequences of our allowing them to be stirred up and maintained, there has occurred a narrowing-down of the radius of our own life, so that in excluding others it is we ourselves who experience exclusion, and the man or woman who tries to 'concentrate entirely on my own life' ends up having little or no life to concentrate upon. The result of being governed by the ego is to make each man or woman a prisoner of his own self-interest, like the prince in the fairy story who was locked up inside a tree.

Why, and how, does this narrowing-down take place? And how is it possible—if it *is* possible—for us to prevent it happening?

---

* James Thurber's famous story, *The Secret Life of Walter Mitty* is such an ego fantasy. And much of the 'stream of consciousness' writing, which was started by the last chapter in James Joyce's *Ulysses*, consists of the musings of different egos. The modern phrase an 'ego trip' conveys a general truth in popular terms.

"Selfishness," Baba tells us, "inevitably leads to dissatisfaction and disappointment, because desires are endless. The problem of happiness is, therefore, the problem of dropping out desires. Desires, however, cannot be effectively overcome through mechanical repression. They can be annihilated only through knowledge. If you dive deep into the realm of thoughts and think seriously for just a few minutes, you will realise the emptiness of desires. Think of what you have enjoyed all these years and what you have suffered. All that you have enjoyed through life is today nil. All that you have suffered through life is also nothing in the present. All was illusory. It is your right to be happy and yet you create your own unhappiness by wanting things. Wanting is the source of perpetual restlessness. If you do not get the thing you wanted, you are disappointed. And if you get it, you want more and more of it and become unhappy. Say, 'I do not want anything' and be happy. As long as man has a body there will be some needs, and it is necessary to meet these needs. But wants are an outcome of infatuated imagination. They must be scrupulously killed if there is to be any happiness. The continuous realisation of the futility of wants will eventually lead you to Knowledge. This Self-Knowledge will give you the freedom from wants which leads to the road to abiding happiness."

Once a man begins to understand that it is his own selfishness which has limited and curtailed his life, then, Baba tells us, "he is heading towards a life of service. At this stage he entertains many good desires. He wants to make others happy by relieving distress and helping them. And though even in such good desires there is often an indirect and latent reference to the self, narrow selfishness has no grip over good deeds. Persistent and continuous performance of good deeds wears out selfishness. Selfishness, extended and expressed in the form of good deeds, becomes the instrument of its own destruction. Selfishness, which in the beginning is the father of evil tendencies, becomes through good deeds the hero of its own defeat. When the evil tendencies are completely replaced by good tendencies, individual selfishness loses itself in universal interest. Goodness is the means by which the soul annihilates its own ignorance."

What makes it supremely difficult for man to understand his own true nature, and to accept the bond which unites him to all other men—indeed to the whole universe—is the state of subjection to the ego in which we live. And the ego, like a computer with an in-built fault, seeks a solution to every problem through false valuation, based on the effort to secure advantage at the expense of others, and to gratify desires which always multiply faster than they can be satisfied.

"The ego," Baba says, "thus represents a deep and fundamental principle of ignorance which is exhibited in always preferring the unimportant to the important.... The establishment of the true ideal is a beginning of right valuation. Right valuation in turn is the undoing of the constructions of the ego, which thrives on false valuation. Any action which expresses the true values of life contributes towards the disintegration of the ego, which is a product of ages of ignorant action. Life cannot be permanently imprisoned within the cage of the ego. It must at some time strive towards the Truth. In the ripeness of evolution comes the momentous discovery that life cannot be understood and lived fully as long as it is made to move round the pivot of the ego. Man is then driven by the logic of his own experience to find the true centre of experience and reorganise his life in the Truth. This entails the wearing out of the ego and its replacement by Truth-consciousness."

The arduous process by which such wearing out and replacement can be achieved is set out fully and inspiringly by Baba in the three-part discourse mentioned earlier in this chapter, and to whose contents and message we have offered no more than an abbreviated introduction.

These three sections on the Ego, with the related 'Discourse on Selfishness', together constitute an exposition so profound, so penetrating in analysis, so closely-knit in argument, so illuminating in the possibilities unfolded for a new approach to life, that if a man were to devote ten years to studying them and seeking to be guided by them, he would be repaid many times over in the expansion of his consciousness and the enrichment of his life.

Chapter 17

SEX, MARRIAGE AND LOVE

BABA DEVOTES THREE separate discourses to these subjects—'The Problem of Sex', 'The Sanctification of Married Life', and 'Love'. They follow one another in that order, though in the original Indian edition, another discourse, 'The Search for God', comes between 'The Sanctification of Married Life' and 'Love'. This is the reverse of the conventional approach: Love-Sex-Marriage or Love-Marriage-Sex would be the expected plan. But Baba does not speak of love as a preliminary to something else. It is itself the highest peak to which, through intense effort, humanity can hope to attain. "Love," he tells us, "is no game for weaklings." Born out of sacrifice, developed through sustained struggle with the ego, divine in essence, and the sole purpose of our life on earth: "It is for love that the whole universe sprang into existence and it is for the sake of love that it is kept going." So Baba begins not with love, but with sex, and goes directly into his subject:

> Sex is one of the most important problems with which we are confronted. It is one of the 'givens' in human nature, and like everything else in life, comes to be considered through the opposites created by the limited mind. Just as mind tries to fit life into a scheme of alternatives such as joy/sorrow, good/bad, attraction/repulsion, so, in relation to sex, it tends to think of indulgence and repression as alternatives from which there is no escape, thus obliging man to accept one or the other. Yet he cannot whole-heartedly accept either, for when he tries repression he is dissatisfied and longingly thinks of indulgence. Equally, when he tries indulgence he becomes conscious of his bondage to the senses. Thus searching for happiness and freedom, the mind gets caught up in the equally disappointing opposites of indulgence and repression. However, in spite of alternate and repeated disappointment, the mind usually does not renounce the root cause of unhappiness

which is craving, because, while experiencing disappointment in repression, it is easily susceptible to the false promise of gratification, and while experiencing disappointment in gratification, is equally susceptible to the false promise of mechanical repression. This is like moving within a cage. The need for indulgence or mechanical repression arises because the nature of craving is not clearly grasped. When the mind becomes fully aware of the inevitable bondage and suffering entailed by craving, it begins voluntarily to disburden itself of craving through intelligent understanding. Mind turns to mechanical repression because of disappointment, but it turns to internal and spontaneous renunciation of craving because of disillusionment or awakening.

Disappointment, as we can usually see in others' cases if not always in our own, is an emotional state rooted in self-pity. It implies that we have been 'let-down' in our justified expectations, and these may well succeed if we try again, or in a new direction, which is exactly what we all tend to do in our sex lives. Disillusion, however, is based on reason, and what it tells us is that we have been following illusion and that, so long as we choose to delude ourselves, we cannot possibly find what we are seeking. It is not therefore related to self-pity but to self-reproof. Disillusion leads to an awakening, awakening to the need to face reality, with the recognition in this case that, since it is craving which was the source of self-deception, it is craving which must be got rid of.

The situation of a man planted between the alternatives of indulgence and repression—and hazily beginning to perceive that he can find peace in neither—has been eloquently expressed from what might seem an unlikely source. Lord Byron wrote from Italy to his friend John Hobhouse: "I feel and I feel it bitterly that a man should not consume his life at the side and on the bosom of a woman . . . that even the recompense—and it is much—is not enough . . . but I have neither the strength of mind to break the chain nor the insensibility which would deaden its weight. I cannot tell what will become of me."

Many men have felt, and feel, as Byron felt, and vacillate or have vacillated between two extremes, 'not knowing what will become' of them. And when we look at life from a broader standpoint, there is the same picture of vacillation. The age into which we have lately moved is known to us as 'the permissive age', but it might equally well be called an age of indulgence. There have in the course of history been many periods of indulgence or permissiveness just as there have been many periods of repression. The one, as Baba has shown, is both the cause and consequence of the other. The pendulum swings across the centuries just as it swings in the smaller time-scale of our own lives. The present period of indulgence follows upon a period of repression, the Victorian age, in which the normal sexual restraints and taboos were reinforced by many that were abnormal and excessive. Many older people alive today were brought up in this repressive atmosphere and suffered, often severely, from its restrictiveness. As a result the belief has spread that problems over sex only arise because the 'natural' self has been inhibited. If this natural self were allowed full freedom from an early age—the argument runs—there would be no inhibition and no suffering but a completely free enjoyment of sexuality, which would lead sooner or later, it is assumed, to love and happy marriage, without the need for special effort on our part, but simply 'in the course of nature'.

What Baba now tells us, however, is the very opposite of this agreeable fantasy. Promiscuity, he says, does not lead to freedom but to bondage, and bondage to lust which is more potent than any drug.

> In promiscuity the temptation to explore the possibilities of mere sex is formidable. But if the mind tries to understand sex through increasing the scope of sex, the delusions to which it becomes a prey are as endless as the scope of sex itself. Only by the maximum restriction of the scope of mere sex can the aspirant arrive at any real understanding of the values attainable through the gradual transformation of sex into love. Love is different from lust. In lust there is reliance on the object of sense and consequent spiritual subordination of the soul to it, but love puts the soul into direct relation with the reality behind the form. Therefore lust is experienced as heavy, and love as being light. In lust there is a narrowing down of life; in love an expansion of being. To have loved one soul is like adding its life to your own. Your life is, as it were, multiplied and you virtually live in two centres. If you love the whole world, you vicariously live in the whole world, but in lust there is an ebbing down of life and a sense of hopeless dependence on a form which is regarded as another. Thus, in lust there is

an accentuation of separateness and suffering, but in love the feeling of unity and joy. Lust is dissipation, love is recreation. Lust is a craving of the senses, love is the expression of the spirit. Lust seeks fulfilment, but love experiences fulfilment. In lust there is excitement but in love there is tranquillity.

Again, in promiscuity the suggestions of lust are necessarily the first to present themselves to the mind, and the individual is doomed to react within the limitation of this initial perversion and thus close the door to deeper experiences. But truth cannot be grasped by skipping over the surface of life and multiplying superficial contacts. It requires the preparedness of mind which can centre its capacities upon selected experiences. This process of discrimination between lower and higher, and the transcendence of the lower in favour of the higher, is made possible through whole-hearted concentration and a genuine interest in life. Such concentration and interest is impossible when the mind becomes a slave to the habit of wandering between many possible objects of similar experience.

Baba's theme of the enslaving power of sensuality pursued for its own sake cannot fail to awaken echoes in many hearts. The sensual life, inevitably one of promiscuity in greater or less degree, is based on a double delusion, that happiness can be found through the multiplication of desires and their satisfaction; and, secondly, that it is possible to remain in control of desires to which one continually gives way, though commonsense tells us this is impossible. The same theme, familiar throughout art and literature, is to be found most potently in myth, that great repository of the world's unconscious knowledge. Medusa, the Gorgon, whose head, beautiful but horrible, turned everyone who looked on it to stone, was represented with the serpents of desire around her face instead of hair, and with serpents also at her girdle. In more recent times the story known to everyone is that of Don Juan, whose name has passed into our everyday language. There are many versions of his story, but in most Don Juan, after a life devoted to seduction, betrays a girl of noble family, and then kills the father who is seeking to avenge her. Some time later, seeing a stone effigy of the father on his tomb, he flippantly asks it to dinner. The effigy, representing Don Juan's humanity now turned to stone, does indeed come to dinner, and this visit proves to be the harbinger of Juan's death. In both myths the implication is the same. Lust, pursued for its own sake, inevitably leads to callousness towards others and their claims. So in time it separates a man or woman from his own humanity. The capacity to feel is lost in the pursuit of sensation, and the victimiser, become his own victim, is turned inwardly to stone.

From a consideration of prosmiscuity and its effects, Baba turns to a comparison with married life. Here, too, sex is involved, but, he says,

> Sex in marriage is entirely different from sex outside marriage. In marriage the impressions of lust are much lighter and more easily removed. Married life makes many demands on both partners for mutual adjustment and understanding, and creates problems not originally expected. In married life two souls become linked in so many ways that they are called upon to tackle the whole complex problem of personality rather than that created by some isolated desire. Promiscuous sex attempts to separate the problem of sex from other needs of the developing personality, and to solve it in isolation from them. Although this kind of solution might seem easy, it turns out to be utterly superficial. It has the further disadvantage of side-tracking the aspirant from attempting the real solution. In married life there is ample room for varied experience, with the result that the different tendencies latent in the mind begin to organise around the crystallised scheme of married life. This organisation of varied purposes not only provides an unlimited field for discrimination between higher and lower values, but also creates the tension between them required to call forth effective and intelligent sublimation.
>
> Married life brings an intensification of most human problems. As such it becomes the rallying ground for the forces of bondage as well as for those of freedom, for the factors of ignorance as well as for the factors of light. As married life tends to be determined by mixed motives and considerations, it inevitably invites opposition between the higher and lower self. Such opposition is necessary for the wearing out of the lower self and the dawning of the True Self. Married life develops so many points of contact between two souls that severance of all connection would mean deranging the whole tenor of life. Since this difficulty of breaking away from one another encourages inner readjustment, marriage affords an opportunity for the souls to establish a lasting understanding which can cope with the most complex and delicate situations.

Today it is sometimes argued that marriage is 'out-of-date' and has no place in the modern world. Free and independent spirits, it is suggested, should live freely and independently, pairing and parting without obligation. Divorce should require nothing more than the consent of both parties that their arrangement is now ended; financial and other details can be worked out by lawyers acting for both sides. Apart from the question of children, whose need for stability and parental love is ignored under such a system, there is the fact stressed by Baba that no serious relationship has the opportunity to develop if the tie can be broken with a word or at a whim. Some cases of grievous hardship are indeed produced by any marriage laws, but the institution itself represents far more than a mere legal framework; it stands for nothing less than the longing and aspiration of men and women to reach together a deeper understanding and experience of life than either could attain alone.

"The spiritual value of married life," Baba goes on to say,

> is directly related to the nature of the factors determining its daily course. If based on shallow considerations, it can deteriorate into a partnership in selfishness aimed against the rest of the world. If inspired by lofty idealism, it can rise to a fellowship which not only calls forth increasing sacrifices for each other, but actually becomes a medium through which the two souls can offer their united love and service to the whole family of humanity. When married life is thus brought into line with the Divine Plan for the evolution of the individual, it becomes a blessing for the children who are its fruit and who absorb a spiritual atmosphere from the very beginning.
>
> The married life of the parents is enriched in turn by the presence of the children. Children give parents an opportunity for expressing and developing spontaneous love in which sacrifice becomes easy and delightful, and the part played by children is of tremendous importance for the spiritual advancement of the parents themselves. It therefore follows that when children make their appearance they ought to be welcomed wholeheartedly.

We come at this point to what Baba has to say on birth control and the widespread movement for population control based on birth control techniques. Even the best-intentioned may flinch at the high and uncompromising standard Baba sets, while at the same time being impressed by the force of logic behind the spiritual values he brings to our attention. He begins:

> In view of the claims children have on married lives, the present birth control movement deserves careful and critical examination. The question must not be considered from the point of view of any one special, therefore limited, interest, but from that of the ultimate well-being both of the individual and society. The right opinion in this, as in all respects, must be based on spiritual considerations. While birth control is right in its aim of securing the regulation of the population, it is disastrously unfortunate in the choice of means. The regulation of child-bearing is often desirable for personal and social reasons. Uncontrolled breeding intensifies the struggle for existence and may bring about a social order where ruthless competition becomes inevitable. Apart from creating responsibilities for parents they may be unable to discharge, it becomes an indirect cause of poverty, crime and war.
>
> However the purely physical means generally advocated by the supporters of birth control are objectionable, and remain, from the spiritual point of view, indefensible. Though advocated on humanitarian grounds, they are mostly used to serve selfish ends and to avoid the responsibility of bearing and bringing up children. Furthermore, since the physical consequences of yielding to lust can so successfully be avoided through these means, those who have not begun to awaken to higher values have no incentive to be moderate in gratification, and can thus become slaves to animal passion.
>
> From the spiritual point of view, therefore, birth control must be effected through mental control and nothing else. Physical means are under no circumstances advisable, even when a person seeks to use them merely as a provisional and secondary aid, without intending to ignore the ideal of developing mental control. Though he may remain for some time under the delusion that he is trying to develop mental control, he is in fact gradually losing it. In short, mental power is necessarily undermined by reliance on physical means, which is also positively disastrous for spiritual advancement. This applies to spiritual aspirants in particular, but also to all human beings, because all are, potentially, spiritual aspirants.
>
> Mental control secures the humanitarian purposes which inspire birth control and keeps clear of the spiritual disasters

entailed by the use of physical means. Mental control is not only useful for regulating the number of children, but is also indispensable for restoring man to his divine dignity and spiritual well-being. Only through its wise exercise is it possible for man to rise from passion to peace, from bondage to freedom, from animality to purity.

Through this process of sublimation, lust ultimately gives place to deep love. It is bound to be gradual, and in cases of failure in practising control, the couple must allow nature to take its own course rather than interfere with it through artificial means. They must cheerfully welcome the consequences and be prepared to shoulder the responsibility of bringing up children. In a properly adjusted marriage there need be no injustice in the distribution of parental responsibility. If both are truly conscious of their mutual responsibility, inconsiderateness will give way to co-operative endeavour to attain full mental control. By the mutual sharing of joys and sorrows, the partners march on from one spiritual triumph to another, from deep love to ever deeper love, till the limited love of the initial period is entirely replaced by a self-giving and expansive love. In fact, through the intelligent handling of marriage, a person may traverse so much of the spiritual path that it needs only a touch by the Master to raise him into the sanctuary of eternal life.

For the man or woman truly in search of inner freedom, the alternative to married life is celibacy. "It must be borne in mind," Baba says,

> that the life of freedom is decidedly nearer to the life of restraint than to the life of indulgence. Hence for the aspirant, if restraint comes easily, celibacy is preferable to married life. Such restraint, however, is difficult for most persons and sometimes impossible, so for them married life is decidedly more helpful. Just as celibacy requires and calls forth many virtues, so married life in turn nourishes the growth of many spiritual qualities of the utmost importance. The value of celibacy lies in the habit of restraint and the sense of detachment and independence it gives. The value of marriage lies in lessons of mutual adjustment and the sense of unity with the other.
>
> For the celibate as well as for the married person the path of inner life is the same. When drawn by the Truth the

aspirant longs for nothing else, and as Truth increasingly comes within his ken, he gradually disburdens himself of craving. Whether in celibacy or marriage, he is no longer swayed by the deceptive promises of indulgence or mechanical repression and so practices internal and spontaneous renunciation of craving until he is freed from the deceptive opposites.

It may seem that in the foregoing passages Baba is setting before us an ideal higher than we can hope to attain. Few aspire to reach Truth through celibacy, and not many couples look upon marriage as a spiritual path. As a Perfect Master, Baba impresses on us the need to regard every activity in life, not from the angle of advantage or enjoyment, but always from that of the ultimate well-being both of the individual and society, that is, from the spiritual point of view. However in his contact with individuals, particularly those who were guilty or distressed, Baba showed the utmost gentleness and understanding. His concern was always with the heart and love: "I am not concerned," he said, "with people's sins." And when a woman, who regarded herself as, in her own word 'naughty', came to see him, Baba made her sit quietly by his side for a minute or two. Then, "Why think like that?" he asked her, "and why worry about it? It is good to think of our defects to improve them, but don't always worry about defects."

On one of his first visits to London, two young men, artists in different fields, living together, were anxious to come and see Baba. But in view of all they had heard about him, they approached in a state of inner trepidation. As they came towards him, Baba held out his arms and with a twinkle in his eye, addressed them with the one-word enquiry, "Chums?"

Having shown, in his discourse on marriage, the heights to which human love can attain, Baba goes on to show that such perfected human love can lead on to something greater still, to which he gives the name 'pure love', and this in turn to 'divine love' in which man becomes one with God.

Pure love is the bloom of spiritual perfection. Human love is so tethered by limiting conditions that the spontaneous appearance of pure love from within becomes impossible. Pure love arises in the heart of the aspirant in response to the descent of grace from the Master. When pure love is first received as a gift of the Master it becomes lodged in the consciousness of the aspirant like a seed in favourable soil. In the course of time the seed develops into a plant and then into a full-grown tree.

Lest it be assumed that we have to go looking for this 'Master' in order to have grace descend upon us, Baba has made clear elsewhere, and again in the passage which immediately follows, that our task is not to wander round in search of such a being, but to prepare ourselves inwardly to receive his grace. "As soon as the disciple is ready the grace of the Master descends, for the Master, who is the ocean of divine love, is always on the lookout for the soul in whom his grace will fructify." And in the passage just concluded, his use of the phrase "pure love from within" shows he is referring to the Eternal Master Within, namely God, with whom Baba is One, and with whom we, as he is constantly telling us, are, in our True Selves, also One. Hence his reiterated "You and I are not We but One."

He continues,

> The descent of the grace of the Master is conditioned, however by the preliminary spiritual preparation of the aspirant. This preparation for grace is not complete until the aspirant has built into his psychic make-up some divine attributes. When a person avoids backbiting and thinks more of the good points in others than of their bad ones, can practise supreme tolerance and desires the good of others even at the cost of his own, he is ready to receive the grace of the Master. The kind of love awakened by the Master is a rare privilege. The mother who is willing to sacrifice all and to die for her child, the martyr who is prepared to give up his life for his country, are indeed supremely noble, but they have not necessarily tasted this pure love born through the grace of the Master. Even the great yogis who, sitting in caves and mountains are completely absorbed in deep *samadhi* (superconscious bliss), do not necessarily have this precious love.
>
> This love is more valuable than any other stimulus. It not only combines in itself the merits of all the disciplines, but excels them all in its efficacy to lead the aspirant to his goal. All his thoughts turn away from the self and come to be exclusively centred on the Divine Beloved.
>
> Through the intensity of this evergrowing love he eventually breaks through the shackles of the self and becomes united

with the Beloved. This is the consummation of love. When love has thus found its fruition it has become divine.

Divine love arises after the disappearance of the individual mind and is free from the trammels of individual nature. In human love the duality of the lover and the beloved persists, but in divine love the lover and the Beloved become one. At this stage the aspirant has stepped out of the domain of duality and becomes one with God, for divine love *is* God. When the lover and the Beloved are one, that is the end and the beginning.

Love is the reflection of God's unity in the world of duality. It constitutes the entire significance of creation. If love is excluded from life, all the souls in the world assume complete externality to each other, and the only possible relations and contacts in such a loveless world are superficial and mechanical. It is because of love that the contacts and relations between individual souls become significant. It is love which gives meaning and value to all the happenings in the world of duality, but it is at the same time a standing challenge to duality. As love gathers strength, it generates creative restlessness and becomes the main driving power of that spiritual dynamic which ultimately succeeds in restoring to consciousness the original unity of being.

Chapter 18

THE SOUL'S JOURNEY THROUGH CREATION (1)

THE WELL-KNOWN physicist, the late Dr J. Robert Oppenheimer, in his 1953 Reith Lectures, spoke of man's, "Two ways of thinking—the way of time and history: the way of eternity and timelessness," stating that "Both are part of man's effort to comprehend the world in which he lives. Neither is comprehended in the other, nor reducible to it. They are ... complementary views, each supplementing the other, neither telling the whole story."

Lovingly aware of the human dilemma of being caught between the 'Absolute' and the 'relative', Baba, using all the authority of his claimed and acclaimed Perfect Mastery and Avatarship, presents 'God', the 'Absolute', the 'Oversoul' and 'Soul', the 'Infinite' as unarguable Realities of Transcendental Eternity and Timelessness. Likewise, he deals with incarnation, reincarnation, evolution, involution, Karma, religion, metaphysics, science as unarguable aspects of space/time experience. He presents them as being purposive in intent, stating with all the eloquence and power of his Transcendental Being, that they contribute to the Divine Plan, the motivational driving force of which is Divine Love.

For those to whom only the knowable world of what they believe to be time/space reality is acceptable, the word 'divine' will be meaningless. So too, for them, may be this chapter and the ones which follow. Even those who are prepared to be more open to unexplored possibilities may find great resistances welling up in them.

Baba's Discourse entitled 'The Search For God' begins—"Most persons do not even suspect the existence of God, so naturally are not keen about God. . . . God either exists or does not exist. If He exists search for Him is amply justified. If He does not exist there is nothing to lose by seeking Him. But man does not usually turn to a real search for God as a matter of voluntary and joyous enterprise. He has to be driven to this search by disillusionment with the things of this world...."

Even those who have started on this search may find much of these chapters hard going. Baba's thought, however, even when dealing with the profoundest issues, is always logical; his expression simple and direct. The difficulty lies in the scale of his subject and the nature of his theme; there is never any confusion in what he says. Except for some linking words and sentences, Baba's own words have been used throughout, but condensed and rearranged from different Discourses and from the Appendix of C. B. Purdom's *The Perfect Master*—which was specially given to Purdom by Baba. It will be appreciated that it is not possible within the scope of such a book as this to deal with any aspect of the teaching at length. We give what have been for us the highlights, though not necessarily in logical sequence.

A question likely to come into the mind after reading this chapter's title is, "What is the nature of the 'soul'?" Baba tells us—"In reality, the soul is identical with the Oversoul (the English equivalent of the Sanskrit term *Paramatman* meaning God, the One, Infinite and Eternal whose cosmic and universal life embraces all). Thus, the soul exists eternally in and with the Oversoul in an inviolable unity. In the beginning, though, the soul was unconscious of its Oneness with the Oversoul and its Infinite Peace, Bliss, Knowledge and Power. In order to realise and experience this, therefore, it had to evolve consciousness."

Baba states—"The sole purpose of creation is that the soul should be able to enjoy the Infinite state of the Oversoul consciously." In his Discourse on Love he tells us—"It is for love that the whole universe sprang into existence and it is for the sake of love that it is kept going."

To help us towards some understanding of how manifested life arose, Baba gives us this remarkable analogy. "Just as a wave going across the surface of a still ocean creates innumerable bubbles, so the impetus in the Absolute to become conscious of itself creates myriads of individual souls out of the indivisible infinity of the Oversoul. Within the undifferentiated being of the Absolute is born a mysterious point through which comes forth the variegated manyness of creation. The vasty deep which, a fraction of a second before was icy-still, is astir with the life of innumerable frothy selves who secure their separateness in definite size and shape through self-limitation within the foamy surface of the ocean." It will be recalled that Genesis, the first book of the Old Testament, opens with these words—"In the beginning God created the heaven and the earth. And the earth was without form, and void; and darkness was upon the face of the deep. And the Spirit of God moved upon the face of the waters."

Explaining that his image is only an analogy, Baba is concerned that we should not make the mistake of deducing that some real change takes place in the Absolute "since any real change would be a negation of its Absoluteness. The change implied is not an ontological change, nor one in the being of Absolute Reality. It is only an apparent change." In one sense, a sort of expansion of the Absolute, through which act the Infinite, being without consciousness, seeks to attain its consciousness. As this expansion of Reality is effected through its self-limitation into various forms of life, we have the paradox that it is at one and the same time both an expansion and a contraction. An expansion in the interest of consciousness; a contraction because of self-limitation. Hence Baba's insistence that—"The all-abounding Absolute is, and will ever remain, the substratum of all the individual souls", and that—"The Oversoul forever remains the same without suffering any real expansion, contraction, increment or decrement, despite there coming into existence its apparent differentiation into many individual souls. . . ."

> There is only one being in reality and it is the Universal Soul. You are the Universal Soul. You are infinite. You are really everywhere, but you do not know your true nature. Were you to look within and experience your own soul in its true nature, you would realise that you are infinite and beyond all creation. But you identify yourself with your body, experience yourself as limited and therefore consider yourself limited. But the infinite belongs to the non-dual order of being. It therefore cannot suffer any increase through additions; nor can it suffer any decrease through subtractions. Nothing can be added to it; nothing can be taken from it. It is all-inclusive, immeasurable, indivisible and integral. And you are infinite.

Baba is here restating the basic truth of all religions, which is summed up for most Westerners in the words of Christ—"The Kingdom of God is within you." It also makes crystal clear Baba's statement that "Selfishness is born of fundamental ignorance about one's own true nature."

Incidentally, this vision of the Universal Soul underlying all creation provides an answer to the classic dilemma of philosophers in the seventeenth and eighteenth centuries, from Descartes, through Locke, Berkeley and Hume. This might be summed up as: "Since all we can know are the impressions conveyed to us by our senses, how can we be sure that these are not deceiving us, and that there exists a 'real world' corresponding in any way to what we suppose we know?" Baba's statement is foreshadowed in the answer given by Berkeley* as a deduction: "... all the choir of heaven and the furniture of the earth, in a word all those bodies which compose the mighty frame of the world, have not any subsistence without a mind... their *being* (esse) is to be perceived and known... consequently so long as they are not actually perceived by me, or do not exist in my mind or that of any other *created spirit*, they must either have no existence at all, *or else subsist in the mind* of some eternal spirit."

The inevitable question which now arises is—"How does the soul become caught up in 'illusion'? How did the Formless, Infinite and Eternal Soul come to experience itself as having form, as being finite, limited and destructible? How did it come to think of itself as the world of nature? In other words, what is the cause of the cosmic illusion in which the soul finds itself?"

To realise the Oversoul which is One, Indivisible, Real and Infinite, the soul had to become conscious. The evolution of consciousness required the duality of a subject and object, the centre of consciousness, the ego and the environment, namely, the world of forms, all of which is within the limitations of time. The soul's first consciousness however, is not of God but of the universe, not of the Eternal Absolute but of the relative and transitory. Thus the soul, instead of realising the Oversoul, becomes involved in the cosmic illusion. Though in reality Infinite, it experiences itself as finite, so comes to believe itself to be finite. In other words, with the development of consciousness the soul does not become conscious of its own true nature, but of its shadow, the phenomenal world.

The noted biologist and naturalist, Konrad Lorenz, author of

---

* George Berkeley (1685–1753), philosopher and Irish bishop, wrote his famous work *The Principles of Human Knowledge* at the age of twenty-six.

the stimulating book *On Aggression*, has shown through his experiments with geese, that the gosling—and indeed the young of other birds and beasts—takes the first living creature its eyes light on after birth or breaking through its shell, to be its parent. A goose can accept a man as its mother. Equally, human beings believe the phenomenal world of illusion into which they are born, to be a world of reality.

Baba constantly stressed the value of science and its practical attainments, explaining—"It is a mistake to look upon science as anti-spiritual. Science is a help or hindrance to spirituality according to the use to which it is put. Just as true art expresses spirituality, so science, when properly handled, can become a medium for the soul to know itself. The balanced progress of humanity can be assured only if science and religion proceed hand in hand...."

It is less than a hundred and twenty years since Charles Darwin shattered both the scientific and religious establishments of his day with the theory of evolution, now largely accepted by those same establishments. To scientific knowledge of the evolution of forms, from the simplest to the most complex, Baba adds knowledge of the evolution of consciousness, telling us that:

> The history of evolution is the history of a gradual development of consciousness. In order to become conscious of the phenomenal world, the soul has to assume some form for experiencing it. The first gross form it assumes for effecting this is that with which evolution begins—namely stone—the most undeveloped. Consciousness at this stage, being of the most partial and rudimentary type, is hopelessly inadequate to fulfil the purpose of creation which was to enable the Oversoul to know itself. Whatever little capacity for illumination consciousness has in the stone phase is derived from the Oversoul, and not from the body of the stone. But consciousness is unable to enlarge its scope independently of the body of the stone because the Oversoul first identifies with consciousness, then through it to the stone form. Since further development is arrested by the inert body of the stone, evolution of higher forms of manifestation becomes necessary. The development of consciousness has to proceed side by side with the evolution of the body by which it is conditioned. Therefore, the will-to-be conscious inherent in the Oversoul seeks, by divine determination, a progressive evolution of the vehicles of expression.

Thus the Oversoul forges for itself a new vehicle of expression in the metal form. Even at this stage, consciousness is very rudimentary, so has to get itself transferred to still higher forms of vegetation and trees, in which there is an appreciable advance in the development of consciousness through the maintenance of the vital processes of growth, decay and reproduction. Emergence of a still more developed form becomes possible when the Oversoul seeks manifestation through the instinctive life of insects, birds and animals who are fully aware of their bodies and of their surroundings, who develop a sense of self-protection and aim at establishing mastery over their environment. In the higher animals, intellect or reasoning also appears, but its working is strictly limited by the play of their instincts, such as the instinct of self-preservation and the instinct for the care and preservation of the little ones.

Finally the Oversoul takes the human form. In this the capacity of reasoning has the widest range of activity and is unlimited in scope, with complete awareness of the self and the environment.... The will-to-be-conscious with which evolution started, therefore, can now be effected in the 'Man-potential-God' state, which is the fairest flower of humanity.

We may well at first find it difficult to accept that there is any degree of consciousness, however slight, in rock or stone. It was at one time unacceptable to believe that plants or trees possess some limited degree of consciousness, can suffer shocks or traumas, respond to the care or presence of certain people rather than to others—yet the knowledge that they do so was forming part of man's everyday picture of life long before it was allowed scientific respectability. We talk of people having 'green fingers', meaning that the plants they grow fare better than those grown by other people. Equally every farmer knows that some men 'get on with' cattle or sheep in a way quite unrelated to intelligence or general ability, indeed it is sometimes those regarded as 'slow-witted' or in some way handicapped who are most successful in such work. We also tend, in our everyday thought, to look upon gardening, farm-work, and the care of crops and animals, as beneficial or healing activities. They are recommended, without scientific explanation but on a basis of general acceptance, as likely to benefit those of us who are distressed or disturbed.

THE SOUL'S JOURNEY THROUGH CREATION (I)

The common man's experience of life, it would seem, often gives him in simplified form truth which is inaccessible to the learned or to theoreticians. The British have been ridiculed, and we constantly ridicule ourselves, for our twin passions of gardening and the keeping of domestic pets. Yet these 'passions' have not only helped millions of us in an increasingly artificial society to maintain some contact with the natural world, but have contributed to man's growing awareness that all creation is interdependent in a way that is none the less real for having hitherto been inexplicable. Over the last fifty, and particularly over the last twenty, years man is coming to realise that he must accept full responsibility for this planet and for every kind of life upon it, and that to allow living creatures to be exterminated, and the environment shared by them and us to be polluted and debased, is not only short-sighted from a material point of view, but also spiritually harmful; that is, we are degraded in our own sight for allowing it to happen.

In telling us that "the history of evolution is the history of a gradual development of consciousness" which "has to proceed side by side with the evolution of the body by which it is conditioned," Baba has made plain the nature of that tie which unites the whole of creation with ourselves. Over the last century and a half since Darwin's day, we had come already to accept that man's physical body evolved by a process of imperceptible change out of the most primitive forms; we have also become aware that traces of our fish and animal past are to be observed in our physical conformation and in the pattern of growth of the embryo following conception. What Baba tells us in the Divine Plan is that consciousness has similarly evolved, and that in consequence of this our developed human consciousness is linked, through the impressions of past experience, with the whole range of natural forms.

Chapter 19

THE SOUL'S JOURNEY THROUGH CREATION (2)

WONDERFUL AS IT is to have arrived, in the human form, at full evolutionary development, we have only effected the first half of our journey. Apparently, "Human beings do not have Self-illumination because our consciousness is shrouded in the accumulated imprints of past experience. The will-to-be-conscious with which evolution started has succeeded in creating consciousness, but does not arrive at the knowledge of the Oversoul because the individual soul is impelled to use consciousness for experiencing impressions, instead of utilising it for experiencing its own true nature as the Oversoul. The experiencing of impressions keeps it confined to the illusion of being a finite body trying to adjust itself in the world of things and persons... thus keeping it within the domain of Maya or duality. For the soul consciously to realise its identity with the Oversoul, consciousness has to be retained and all impressions entirely removed. Though having been contributory to the evolution of consciousness, they have now become impediments to its efficacy in illuminating the nature of the Oversoul. The problem henceforth is not that of evolving consciousness but that of releasing it from impressions."

In the first part of his four-part Discourse on Sanskaras (impressions) Baba tells us that "they are of two types—natural and non-natural... Those which the soul gathers during the period of organic evolution are natural. They come into existence as the soul successively takes up and abandons the various sub-human forms, passing gradually from the apparently inanimate state of stone/metal on up to the human state where there is full development of consciousness." It is the impressions imbibed through the various sub-human form experiences and patterns of behaviour which we are now learning so much about from the ecologists. Very revealing it is too, highlighting, as it now does, Baba's choice of the terms 'natural and non-natural'.

"These natural impressions have to be carefully distinguished from those acquired by the soul after the attainment of the human form, the non-natural ones being cultivated under the moral freedom of consciousness and its accompanying responsibility of choice between good and bad, virtue and vice. Though dependent on the natural ones, they are created under fundamentally different conditions of life and are, in their origin, comparatively recent. This difference in the length of the formative period and the conditions of formation of both, is responsible for the difference in degree of the firmness of their attachment to the soul." We are told that "non-natural impressions are not as difficult to eradicate as natural ones, which have an ancient heritage and are therefore more firmly rooted." Furthermore, we are given the warning that "The obliteration of natural impressions is practically impossible without the grace of a Perfect Master." This tells us more powerfully than anything else could the strength of their attachment.

"This acquisition of impressions may be likened," Baba explains, "to the winding of a piece of string around a stick. The string represents the impressions, and the stick the mind of the individual soul. The winding starts from the beginning of creation, persists through all the evolutionary stages and the human forms. The wound string represents all the impressions—natural and non-natural.

"The impressions constantly being created in human life are due to the multifarious objects and ideas with which consciousness is confronted, bringing about important transformations in consciousness. Beneficial impressions—for example those derived from hearing good music, poetry, from good literature, the visual arts or seeing a beautiful landscape—give feelings of exaltation." One is reminded here of the advice given by Goethe, the great German sage, which was never to let a day pass without listening to a good piece of music, reading a fine poem or piece of prose, or contemplating a beautiful picture. He believed that any one or all of these practices had a heightening and refining effect on one's 'being'.

In the same way, Baba points out, "contact with the personality of a great thinker inspires enthusiasm for and interest in new avenues of thoughts utterly foreign to one's former consciousness. Not only impressions of objects or persons, but also impressions of ideas and superstitions can condition consciousness," and as an illustration of the power of impressions of superstition we are given this dramatic example:

Once upon a time, during the Moghul rule in India, an educated man who was sceptical of stories about ghosts decided to verify them from experience. He had been warned against visiting a certain graveyard on the darkest night of the month, for it was reported to be the habitation of a dreadful ghost who made his appearance whenever an iron nail was hammered into the ground in the precincts of the graveyard. The sceptic, with a hammer in one hand and a nail in the other, walked into the graveyard on the darkest night of the month and chose his spot. The ground was dark, so was his loosely hanging cloak. When he hammered, an end of his cloak became caught up in the nail, and was thus pinned down. Congratulating himself on his apparent success, he tried to rise and depart, but felt a strong pull from the ground as he did so. Panic-stricken, he was unable—owing to the operation of previous impressions—to think of anything except the ghost, and concluded it had at last caught him. The shock was so great that the poor man died of heart failure.

Baba aptly continues—"The power and effect of impressions can hardly be over-estimated. An impression is solidified might, and its inertness makes it immobile and durable. It can become so engraved on the mind of man that, despite his sincere desire and effort to eradicate it, it takes its own time and has a way of working itself into action directly or indirectly." After this we are not surprised to be told that "the mind contains many heterogeneous impressions which, while seeking expression in consciousness, often clash with each other. Hence mental conflict." That "experience is bound to be chaotic and enigmatic, full of oscillations, confusion and complex tangles until consciousness is freed from all impressions, whether of good or bad"; and that "experience can only become truly harmonious when consciousness is emancipated from all impressions", which might be differently expressed in the words, "when the human being has become free from all forms of attachment".

The tremendous scope of impressions is even more powerfully brought home to us when we learn that "impressions can be classified according to the spheres to which they refer, which are of three kinds: 1. gross—enabling the soul to experience the gross world through the gross medium, compelling it to identify with the gross body; 2. subtle—enabling the soul to experience the subtle world through the subtle medium, compelling it to identify with its subtle body; 3. mental—enabling the soul to experience the mental world through the mental medium, compelling it to identify with its mental body." The terms here used, gross, subtle and mental, may be unfamiliar to some readers, so that a few words on this metaphysical subject may help. Esoteric teachings throughout the ages have spoken of man as a potentially three-bodied being—that is, as having a physical body which can be seen and touched; then, in embryo, with the possibility of development, a second finer, non-physical body, not discernible to normal vision but subsisting none-the-less in the desire and energy part of our inner being. Then again, also in embryo, but with the possibility of development, a third and even finer body still—not discernible to the eye but subsisting none-the-less in the mental part of our being. In describing or speaking of something or someone we sometimes use the phrase, "I see it in my mind's eye." Brutishness, callousness, drugs, overindulgence in alcohol and sex, are fatal for these finer bodies, besides having a sadly coarsening effect on the physical body.

Spirit, of course, has no body. The Upanishads, part of India's sacred lore which according to tradition goes back over five thousand years, describes Spirit as being "everywhere, without a body, without a shape, whole, pure, wise, all-knowing, far-shining, self-depending, all-transcending..."

In further explanation about the gross, subtle and mental states of the phenomenal world, Baba continues—"Although all three" (being in the realm of the illusory) "are false, they represent different degrees of falseness. Thus the gross world is farthest from Truth [God]; the subtle world is nearer and the mental world nearest. The soul, of course, is beyond all this. However, owing to its identification of itself with its gross, subtle and mental bodies, and the corresponding states of the illusory world, it becomes unaware of this and so experiences itself as finite and limited. Thus entrenched in Maya's cosmic illusion, the soul has started out on its long journey through illusory space/time/form, all of which it has to experience fully, understand fully, and finally, utterly transcend before it realises the Truth."

Seen from the human standpoint, a tough undertaking you might say. Could we but view it from the transcendental point of view, however, being One with the Absolute, we would see it as Baba sees it. He encourages us thus—"All persons have to pass through the state of bondage, but this period must not be looked upon as a meaningless episode in the evolution of life. One has to experience being bound in order to appreciate freedom. If life had been constantly free, man would have missed the real significance of freedom. To experience spiritual bondage and know intense desire to be free from it, both are a preparation for the full freedom which is to come. Real happiness, which comes through realising God, is worth all the physical and mental suffering of the universe. Then, all suffering is as if it were not. The happiness of God-realisation is self-sustained, eternally fresh and unfailing, boundless and indescribable. It is for this happiness that the world has sprung into existence."

Accepting that Creation, as the means through which consciousness is achieved, is God's loving gift to man, we can perhaps say that the soul's long journey through manifestation to arrival at its ultimate destination, when it can consciously enjoy the Infinite state of the Oversoul, is man's grateful gift to God. "God to Man and Man to God" is the meaningful title Baba gave Purdom for the first edited edition of the Discourses. Surely we have here, too, the explanation of Baba's often repeated "Don't worry. Be happy." "I have come not to teach but to awaken." "You and I are not We but One." Being God-realised and a Perfect Master, he knows that in the transcendental state from which we came and to which we must ultimately return, there is "nothing to worry about"; that all conflict and distress will vanish the moment we awaken to the realisation of the underlying truth of our Oneness with God and with him.

However, before the soul can achieve this blissful transcendental state of union with the Oversoul, it has first to free itself from all the impressions acquired during its ages of evolution, and again during its many earthly incarnations. The problem of deconditioning the mind of impressions is thus infinitely important, so it is not surprising that Baba devotes three parts of his four-part Discourse to their removal. Here we can only briefly indicate what is advocated for this essential task. Under a five-way heading we have the following.

1. *The cessation of new ones.* This consists in putting an end to the ever-renewing activity of creating fresh impressions. Using the analogy of the winding of string around a stick, this amounts to the cessation of the further winding of the string.

2. *The wearing out of the old.* If withheld from expressing themselves in action and experience, existing impressions are gradually worn out. This is comparable to the wearing out of the string at the place where it is.
3. *The unwinding of past ones.* This consists in annulling these by mentally reversing the process which led to their formation. This is like unwinding the string.
4. *The dispersion and exhaustion of some.* If the psychic energy locked up in impressions is sublimated and diverted into other channels, they are dispersed and tend to disappear.
5. *Their wiping out.* This consists in completely annihilating them, which is comparable to cutting the string with a pair of scissors. Their final wiping out can be effected only by the grace of a Perfect Master. Baba points out that "many of the concrete methods of undoing impressions are found to be effective in more than one way, and these five ways are not meant to classify these methods into sharply distinguished types. They represent rather the different principles characterising the psychic processes which take place while impressions are being removed."

The practical means which Baba advocates for the removal of impressions are those which have been advocated, and are still advocated, by every great religion, beginning with renunciation.

Renunciation may be external or internal. External renunciation consists in giving up everything to which the mind is attached. Internal or mental renunciation consists in giving up all cravings, particularly the craving for sensual objects. Spiritual freedom consists in internal renunciation and not in external renunciation; but external renunciation is a great aid in achieving internal renunciation.... Though it is difficult to resist and overcome the influence of surroundings, it is easier to escape from them. Many persons would lead a chaste and straightforward life if they were not surrounded by luxuries and temptations. The renunciation of all superfluous things helps the wearing out of impressions and is therefore contributory to the life of freedom.... Rejection of desires is a preparation for desirelessness or the state of non-wanting which alone can bring about true freedom. Wanting is necessarily binding, whether it is fulfilled or not. When it is fulfilled, it leads to further wanting and thus perpetuates the bondage of the spirit. When it is unfulfilled it leads to disappointment and suffering which, through their impressions, fetter the freedom of the spirit in their own way ... wanting is a state of disturbed equilibrium of mind and non-wanting is a state of stable poise.

More will be said about this in the final chapter, meantime it will be clear that the removal of the impressions assimilated over so vast a span of time, and through such a variety of forms, is likely to be a lengthy process—which brings us to the highly controversial subject of Reincarnation and the Law of Karma. Ordinary—or, if you prefer, extraordinary—common sense should tell us that it is not possible to pass from the human state to the divine in the span of a single life, so we will not waste time, space, energy in defending the doctrine of Reincarnation. Baba devotes seven parts to his Discourse on "Reincarnation and Karma", which we can take as a measure of the importance he attaches to its place in the scheme of things. "In order to experience and finally unwind all impressions, the soul has to reincarnate again and again in the human form. The innumerable human forms through which the soul has to pass are determined by the Law of Karma or the nature of its previous impressions, according to whether they are of virtue or vice, happiness or misery." The biblical saying "As a man sows so shall he reap" becomes apt here.

Baba begins his explanation, as so often, with a point of common understanding and acceptance: "The worldly man completely identifies life with the manifestations and activities of the gross body. For him, therefore, the beginning and end of bodily existence are also the beginning and end of the individualised soul. All his experience seems to testify to the transitoriness of the physical body, and he has often witnessed the disintegration of those physical bodies which were once vibrant with life." However, Baba goes on to explain, "Immortality of the individualised soul is rendered possible by the fact that the individualised soul is not the same as the physical body. It continues to exist with all its impressions in the inner worlds through the medium of its mental and subtle bodies, even after it has discarded the gross body at the time of death. So life through the medium of the gross body is only a *section* of the continuous life of the individualised soul; the other sections of its life have their expression in other worlds."

THE SOUL'S JOURNEY THROUGH CREATION (2)

The description which follows is taken from Parts IV, V, and VI of Baba's Discourse on "Reincarnation and Karma": they are headed "Specific Conditions of an Incarnation", "The Need for Male and Female Incarnations" and "The Operation of Karma through Successive Lives".

For the soul which has once attained human status, the normal course is to go through countless reincarnations in the human form itself. The human form may sometimes be male and sometimes female according to the impressions and spiritual requirements of the soul. The female form has the special prerogative that even Sadgurus and the Avatars have to be born through the female form. The male has the prerogative that the majority of the Sadgurus appear in male form. Women can become saints and Sadgurus, but the Avatar always appears in male form.

The general aids and handicaps of an incarnation are always determined by the specific impressions which the individual soul has accumulated in the past. The needs involved in the further development of the soul are related to the nature of its accumulated impressions. The facilities afforded by a specific incarnation are dependent not only on whether it shall be in the male or female form, but also on whether it takes place in one cycle of existence or another one, and matches the tenor of earthly life either in the Eastern hemisphere or the Western. On the whole, the East has developed more on spiritual lines than on material, with the result that the Eastern mind has a spontaneous aspiration for God. The West, on the whole, has developed more on material lines, with the result that the Western mind has a spontaneous urge towards intellectual and artistic things. . . . But the soul has to experience the material as well as the spiritual aspects of life before it is freed from the fetters of divided life. Therefore the same soul has to incarnate in the East as well as in the West. . . .

The facilities afforded by male and female incarnations are not rigidly invariable. They change according to the cycles of existence as well as to whether the incarnation is in the East or the West. In some ages men are more active and materially-minded than women. In other ages the reverse is true. In the past the women of the East were brave and intellectual. Now in the Eastern hemisphere the average man has greater spiritual inclination than the average woman, just as in the West the average woman of today has greater spiritual inclination than the average man. . . .

Before the soul is set free from all impressions, it assumes numerous male and numerous female forms. If the soul were to incarnate only in the male or only in the female forms, its experience would remain one-sided and incomplete. The duality of experience can be overcome only through understanding, and the understanding of experience is only partial so long as it moves within the limits of only one of the two opposites. . . . The purpose of male and female incarnations is the same as the purpose of evolution itself; it is to enable man to arrive at his own undivided and indivisible existence.

"In the successive incarnations of an individual soul," Baba goes on to say,

there is not only a thread of continuity and identity (manifested in personal memory and revived in the case of advanced souls), but there is also an uninterrupted reign of the law of cause and effect through the persistence and operation of *Karma*. The actions of past lives determine the conditions and circumstances of the present life, and the actions of the present life have their share in determining the conditions and circumstances of future lives. The intermittent incarnations in the gross world are only apparently disconnected. Karma persists as a connecting link and determining factor through the mental body, which remains a permanent and constant factor through all the lives. The law of Karma and its manner of operation cannot be understood so long as the gross body and the gross world are considered to be the only facts of existence. Karmic determination is made possible by the existence of subtle and mental bodies and worlds. . . .

The ego-mind is formed by the accumulated impressions of past experiences and actions; and it is this ego-mind which constitutes the kernel of the existence of the reincarnating individual. The ego-mind, as a reservoir of latent impressions, is the state of the mental body . . . and, seated in the mental body, takes lower bodies according to the impressions stored in it. These impressions determine whether a person will die young or old, whether he will experience health or illness or both, whether he will suffer from physical handicaps like blindness or will enjoy general efficiency of the body, whether he will have a sharp or a dull intellect, whether he will be pure or impure of heart, fickle or steadfast in will and whether he will be immersed in the pursuit of material gains or will seek the inner light of the spirit.... The pleasure and pain experienced in life on earth, the success or failure which attend it, the attainments and obstacles with which it is strewn, the friends and foes who appear in it, all are determined by the Karma of past lives. Karmic determination is popularly designated as 'fate'. Fate, however, is not some foreign and oppressive principle. Fate is man's own creation pursuing him from past lives; and just as it has been shaped by past Karma, it can also be modified, remoulded and even undone through Karma in the present life.

Proper understanding and use of the law of Karma enables man to become master of his own destiny through intelligent and wise action. Each person has become what he is through his own accumulated actions; and it is through his own actions that he can mould himself according to the pattern of his heart, or finally emancipate himself from the reign of Karmic determination which governs him through life and death....

The law of Karma is, in the world of values, the counterpart of the law of cause and effect which operates in the physical world. If there were no law of cause and effect in the physical world there would be chaos; in the same way the moral order of the universe is maintained through the systematic connection between cause and effect in the world of values. In its inviolability the law of Karma is like the other laws of nature. Its operation, however, does not come to the soul as the oppressiveness of some external and blind power, but as something involved in the rationality of the scheme of life. Karmic determination is the condition of true responsibility. It means that a man will reap as he sows. What a person meets with by way of experience is invariably connected with what he does.

If a person has done an evil turn to someone he must accept the penalty for it and welcome the evil rebounding upon himself. If he has done a good turn to someone he must also receive the reward for it and enjoy the good rebounding upon himself. What he does for another he has also done for himself, although it may take time for him to realise that this is exactly so. The law of Karma might be said to be an expression of justice or a reflection of the unity of life in the world of duality.

Since earlier on in this chapter Baba has referred to "the domain of Maya or duality", and again to the cosmic illusion as "Maya's comic illusion", something of what he says on this fascinating and highly complex subject must be given. He devotes four parts to his Discourse on Maya, and starts off thus—"Everyone wants to know and realise the Truth, but Truth cannot be known and realised as Truth, unless ignorance is known and realised as being ignorance. Hence arises the importance of understanding Maya or the principle of ignorance. People read, hear about Maya, but few understand what it really is. . . . It is necessary it be understood as it is—i.e. in its reality. To understand Maya . . . is to know half of the Truth of the universe. Ignorance in all its forms must disappear if the soul is to be established in the state of self-knowledge. Therefore it is imperative for man to know what is false, to know it to be false, and to get rid of the false by knowing it to be false. . . . Falsehood consists in taking the true to be other than what it really is. Falsehood is an error in judging the nature of things.

Part One, from which the preceding is taken, is headed "False Values"; Part Two, "False Beliefs"; Part Three, "Transcending The Falsehoods of Maya"; Part Four, "God and Maya". It is from this fourth part that we take the following excerpts.

How does the false world of finite things come into existence? Why does it exist? It is created by Maya or the principle of ignorance. Maya is not illusion, it is the creator of illusion. Maya is not false, it is that which gives false impressions. Maya is not unreal; it is that which makes the real appear unreal and the unreal appear real. Maya is not duality, it is that which causes duality. Maya cannot be considered as being finite. A thing becomes finite by being limited in time. Maya does not exist in space and cannot be limited by it, because space is itself the creation of Maya. Space and all that it contains, is an illusion and is dependent upon Maya. Nor can it have a beginning or an end in time, because time itself is a creation of Maya. Time is in Maya. Maya is not in time. Time comes into existence because of Maya and disappears when Maya disappears. God is a timeless reality, and the realisation of

God and the disappearance of Maya is a timeless act. For the purposes of intellectual explanation, Maya is best regarded as being both real and infinite, in the same way that God is usually regarded as being both real and infinite. [However] there are difficulties in regarding Maya either as illusory or as ultimately real. If, on the one hand it is regarded as finite, it itself becomes illusory and then cannot account for the illusory world of finite things. It has, therefore, to be regarded as being both real and finite. If, on the other hand, it is regarded as being ultimately real, it itself becomes a second part of the duality of another infinite reality, namely God; and from this point of view Maya actually does seem to become finite and unreal.

Thus all attempts of the limited intellect to understand Maya fall short of true understanding and lead to an impasse. Maya is as unfathomable as God. God is unfathomable, un-understandable; so is Maya unfathomable, un-understandable. So they say, 'Maya is God's shadow. Where a man is, there is his shadow also. So, where God is, there is this inscrutable Maya.'

We can sum up our human situation in a few words. Our prejudices, stemming from ignorance of our true reality, are boundless. They affect our judgements which are nearly always false, being based on false premises. Likewise our assumptions. They are nearly always pathetically limited; our presumptions pitiable in their conceit. That is until we arrive at that painful but illuminating realisation that we know nothing as we ought to know. Job's statement to God after his severe but loving testing by God —"Therefore have I uttered that I understood not; things too wonderful for me, which I knew not."

Chapter 20

THE JOURNEY HOME

IN THE COURSE of the last chapter we referred to what Baba tells us about the immense and conscious effort needed to decondition the mind of its inborn, previously acquired, tendencies. In his three-part Discourse on "The Removal of Sanskaras" (impressions), he lists the means to be employed, renunciation, which includes fasting and solitude; penance, which "consists in augmenting and expressing the remorse which a man feels after realising he has done some wrongful act... mentally reviving the wrongs with severe self-condemnation"; and the withholding of desires from fulfilment, which "implies constant effort to maintain watchful detachment in relation to the alluring opposites of limited experience".

But when dealing with the state of "non-wanting which alone can bring about true freedom", and emphasising that "impressions can only be annulled through the negative assertion of 'No' 'No', 'Neti' 'Neti'—'Not-this' 'Not-this'—Baba constantly reveals, not only his sublime understanding of and compassion for us humans, but also his profound wisdom. "This negative element, though necessarily present in all aspects of asceticism... must come naturally without giving rise to any perversions or further limitations. Trying to coerce the mind to a life of asceticism is of no use. Any forcible adjustment of life on ascetic lines is likely to stunt the growth of some good qualities. When the healthy qualities of human nature are allowed to develop naturally and slowly, they unfold the knowledge of relative values and thereby pave a way for a spontaneous life of asceticism, but any attempt to force or hasten the mind towards an ascetic life is likely to invite reaction."

Baba never demands that we attempt to force the pace of progress, and showed throughout his time on earth an intense awareness and understanding for our human predicament. One of the Western women who accompanied him and his party on vast journeys across India during the 'mast-trips' of the early

1940s "had occasion to wait in the car for a number of mornings at the same spot in a particular town. Each day the same beggar —miserable and destitute as only an Indian beggar can be— would come to her whining for alms. At first she gave him something, but as his demands persisted, she became annoyed and pretended to be asleep when she saw him approaching. Later when she told Baba of the annoying incident, she said: 'I don't know why he persists in coming to me *every day*.' Looking at her seriously, Baba replied: 'He gets hungry every day.' "*

In further explanation of the means by which liberation is to be achieved, Baba points out:

> Although the negative assertion of 'No' 'No' is the only way of unwinding the positive impressions gathered through evolution and human lives, this process does result in the formation of negative ones, which also condition the mind and create new problems. Renunciation of desires does not mean asceticism or a merely negative attitude to life. Any such negation of life would make man inhuman. Divinity is not devoid of humanity; spirituality must make man more human. It is a positive attitude of releasing all that is good, noble and beautiful in man. It also contributes to all that is gracious and lovely in the environment. It does not require the external renunciation of worldly activities or the avoiding of duties and responsibilities. It only requires that, while performing the worldly activities and discharging the responsibilities arising from the individual's specific place and position, the inner spirit remains free from the burden of desires.

> Therefore, whilst the assertion of 'No' 'No' has to be sufficiently powerful to effect the eradication of all physical, subtle and mental impressions, after it has served its purpose, it, too, has to be abandoned. The finality of spiritual experience does not consist of a bare negation. This is limiting it by means of an intellectual concept. The negative formula has to be used by the mind to decondition itself, but it must be renounced before the ultimate goal of life can be attained.

> The ability to remain free from the entanglements of duality is the most essential requirement of unhindered creativity; but this freedom cannot be attained by running away from life for fear of entanglement. This would mean denial of life. The attempt to escape from entanglement implies fear of life. But

* Recorded in *Avatar*, by Jean Adriel.

Spirituality consists in meeting life adequately and fully without being overpowered by the opposites, asserting its dominion over all illusions however attractive or powerful.

Thus we are brought to the profound realisation that "thought has to be made use of in order to overcome the limitations set up by its own movement, but when this is done, 'it' itself has to be given up. This amounts to the process of going beyond the mind which becomes possible through non-identification with 'itself' or 'its desires'."

Arrival at the transcendental state of being beyond mind means, we take it, that the will-to-be-conscious with which evolution started, has now effected its purpose which, according to Baba, is "that the soul should consciously know and enjoy its Infinite state of Oneness with the Oversoul, the One, Infinite and Eternal, whose cosmic and universal life embraces all."

Baba tells us,

Consciously or unconsciously, every living creature seeks one thing. In the lower forms of life and in less advanced human beings, the quest is unconscious. In advanced human beings it is conscious. The object of the quest has many names—happiness, peace, freedom, truth, love, perfection, Self-realisation, God-realisation. Essentially it is a search for all of these, but in a special way. We all have moments of happiness, glimpses of truth, even fleeting experiences of union with God. What we want is to make them permanent, to establish abiding reality in the midst of constant change.

It is a natural desire, based fundamentally on a memory, dim or clear as the individual's evolution may be high or low, of his essential unity with God, for every living thing is a partial manifestation of God, conditioned only by its lack of knowledge of its own true nature. The whole of evolution is, in fact, an evolution from unconscious divinity to conscious divinity, in which God Himself, essentially eternal and unchangeable, assumes an infinite variety of forms, undergoes an infinite variety of experiences and transcends an infinite variety of self-imposed limitations... in which the Unconditioned tests the infinitude of His Absolute Knowledge, Power and Bliss in the midst of all conditions.

From the standpoint of the human creature however, with his limited knowledge, power and capacity for enjoying bliss, evolution is an epic of alternating rest and struggle, joy and sorrow, love and hate until, in the perfected man, God balances the pairs of opposites and transcends duality. Then 'creature' and Creator recognise themselves as one; changelessness is established in the midst of change, eternity is experienced in the midst of time. God knows himself as God unchangeable in essence, infinite in manifestation, ever experiencing the supreme bliss of Self-realisation in continually fresh awareness of Himself by Himself.

This realisation must and can only take place in the midst of life, for it is only in the midst of life that limitation can be experienced and transcended, and that subsequent freedom from limitation can be enjoyed.

Recalling, at this stage, Baba's statement made in connection with the evolvement of the human creature—"The will-to-be-conscious with which evolution started ... can now be effected in the 'Man-potential-God' state, which is the fairest flower of humanity"—now hits our awareness with a new force. The seemingly simple but dynamic phrase 'potential-God state' brings to mind his oft-repeated "The Son of God is in every man, but has to be manifested." Strikingly apparent is the link between Avatar Meher Baba's teaching and that of Avatar Jesus of Nazareth—Jesus Christ, the Christed One, the only-begotten of God the Father. It was Jesus' statement—"I and the Father are One. None cometh to the Father but by me," meaning, we assume, the 'Christ-Son-of-God' state—which so very understandably outraged Jewish orthodoxy and led to the Crucifixion.

Jesus' statement—"What I have done all men can do. What I am, all men can be", reported by Clement of Alexandria, now takes on a totally new dimension of meaning for us, for it brings us back, full circle, to Avatar Meher Baba's twentieth-century statement, "The Son of God is in every man but has to be manifested."

At the 1962 East/West Gathering in Poona, India, Baba gave this talk. Addressing all present as "My dear children," he stated that the gathering was "a coming together of the children of East and West in the house of their Father. All religions of the world proclaim that there is but One God, the Father of all in creation. I am that Father. I have come to remind all people that they should live on earth as the children of the One Father until my Grace awakens them to the realisation that they are all

One without a second; that all divisions, conflicts, hatred are but the shadow-play of their own ignorance. Although all are my children, they ignore the simplicity and beauty of this Truth by indulging in hatreds, conflicts and wars that divide them in enmity, instead of living as one family in their Father's House."

A day or two later, enlarging on this, he added, "If you make me your real Father, all differences and contentions between you, all personal problems in connection with your lives will become dissolved in the Ocean of my Love ... I have been patient and indulgent ... because you have been very young children in my love, and children must have some sort of games to play. But you are now older and beginning to realise that there is greater work ahead of you for you to become mature in my love...."*

The search for the perfect father/mother, the perfect husband/wife, the perfect son/daughter is not a phantasy of immaturity but a deep and unquenchable longing in the hearts of all human creatures, masking the real search which is for the divine being within us all. That we call this 'God' and project it outwards is all part of the divine plan.

In his Discourse "The New Humanity" Baba tells us that, "As in all great critical periods of human history, humanity is now going through the agonising travail of spiritual rebirth. Great forces of destruction seem to be dominant at the moment, but creative forces which will redeem humanity are also being released through several channels. Although the working of these forces is chiefly silent, eventually they are bound to bring about transformations which will make the further spiritual advance of humanity safe and steady. It is all part of the divine plan, which is to give to the hungry and weary world a fresh dispensation of the eternal and only Truth.... When it is recognised that there are no claims greater than those of the universal divine life which, without exception, includes everyone and everything—every nationality, every religion—"love will not only establish peace, harmony and happiness in social, national and international spheres, but will shine in its own purity and beauty.... Divine love will not only bring imperishable sweetness and infinite bliss into personal life, but make possible an era of New Humanity which will learn the art of co-operative and harmonious life; free itself from the tyranny of dead forms and release

---

* Reported more fully on pp. 126-7.

the creative life of spiritual wisdom; it will shed all illusions and become established in the Truth; it will enjoy peace and abiding happiness; be initiated in the Life of Eternity."

The perfection we all long for and seek, in whatsoever form we are envisaging it, "Does not belong to God as God, nor does it belong to man as man; but we get perfection when man becomes God or when God becomes man. This is what happens when man gives up the illusion of being finite and attains Godhood by realising his divinity. God's perfection is revealed only when he manifests himself as man. Thus we have perfection when the finite transcends its limits and realises its infinity, or when the Infinite gives up its supposed aloofness and becomes man. In both cases, the finite and the Infinite do not stand outside each other. When there is a happy and conscious blending of the finite and the Infinite, we have Perfection."

We have completed the journey. We have come home.

Avatar Meher Baba. Ki Jai. Ki Jai. Ki Jai.

A SHORT BIBLIOGRAPHY

There are said to be more than a hundred books devoted to Meher Baba, but many of these consist of sayings or extracts from the longer books. Anyone wishing to know more about Baba may find the following short list useful. For convenience, books have been grouped under 'Life' and 'Teaching', but those classified under the former heading all include more or less of the latter.

LIFE

The Perfect Master by C. B. Purdom. Williams and Norgate, 1937. The story of Baba's life up to 1936.

The God-Man by C. B. Purdom. George Allen and Unwin, 1964. This includes "The Perfect Master", but carries the story on up to 1962. Lately republished by Sheriar Press Inc., South Carolina, U.S.A.

Avatar by Jean Adriel. J. F. Rowny Press, California, 1947. A personal narrative going up to the year 1943. Republished John F. Kennedy University Press, Berkeley, 1971.

Listen, Humanity by Meher Baba, narrated and edited by D. E. Stevens. Dodd, Mead and Co., New York, 1957. Part I is the account by Don E. Stevens, of a gathering of Baba's followers in India in November 1955. Part II gives extracts from Baba's teaching, with information by Baba himself, particularly about his early life.

Meher Baba, Family Letters, 1956–1969 by Manija Sheriar Irani. Soc. for Avatar Meher Baba, New York, 1969. These letters, sent out by Baba's sister Mani to followers all over the world, provide the only continuous record for his last years.

Meher Baba's Last Sahavas by Dr H. P. Bharucha. Published by himself from Navsari, India, 1969. This 50-page pamphlet is a first-hand record of the week of Baba's lying-in-state.

The Wayfarers by William Donkin, with a foreword by Meher

Baba. Adi K. Irani for Meher Publications, India, 1948. The extraordinary record of Baba's work with the 'masts' or God-mad.

TEACHING

Discourses by Meher Baba, in five vols. First published 1939, from Ahmednagar, India. Reprinted several times but now out of print.
God to Man and Man to God. A one-vol. edition of the Discourses, edited by C. B. Purdom. Victor Gollancz Ltd., 1955.
Discourses by Meher Baba, in three vols. (paperback). Edited by Ivy Oneita Duce and Don E. Stevens. Sufism Reoriented Inc, 1967, and frequently reprinted.
God Speaks, the Theme of Creation and Its Purpose, by Meher Baba. Dodd, Mead and Co., New York, 1955. Revised and enlarged edition, 1973.
Civilisation or Chaos by I. H. Conybeare. Chetana Ltd., 34 Rampart Row, Bombay 1, India, 1959. A study of the world crisis in the light of Eastern metaphysics.
Stay With God by Francis Brabazon. Garuda Books, Queensland, Australia, 1959. A poetic record of a month's stay with Baba, expanding out into an analysis of world conditions and a vision of the future.

*   *   *

There are currently three magazines devoted to Meher Baba:

The Awakener. Quarterly, edited by Filis Frederick. Published from 038—18th St., Hermosa Beach, California, U.S.A.
Divya Vani (Divine Voice). Monthly, edited by Swami Satya Prakash Udaseen. Distributed by Avatar Meher Baba Mission; 2-26-4, Sri Nagar, Kakinada-3; U.P.; India.
The Glow. Quarterly, edited by Freiny Nalavala and Naosherwan Anzar. Published from 36 Lytton Rd., Dehra Dun, India.

*   *   *

The Meher Baba Association has a Centre in London at 3a, Eccleston Square, London S.W.1.